Library of Congress Cataloging-in-Publication Data

Robinson, Charles M., 1949–
   Texas and the Mexican War : a history and a guide / Charles M. Robinson III
         p.   cm.   —(Fred Rider Cotten popular history series ; no. 16)
"Published . . . in cooperation with the Center for Studies in Texas History at the
University of Texas at Austin" -- T.p. verso.
Includes bibliographical references.
   ISBN 0-87611-192-4 (pbk. : alk. paper)
1. Mexican War, 1846–1848--Texas. 2. Mexican War, 1846–1848--Campaigns. 3.
Texas--History, Military--19th century. 4. Texas--History--1846–1950. 5. Historic
sites--Texas. 6. Texas--History, Local. I. Title. II. Series.
E409.5.T45R63   2003
973.6'242'09764—dc22
                                                              2003021202
                                                                   CIP

Number sixteen in the Fred Rider Cotten Popular History Series.

Publication of this book is supported by a grant from the Summerfield G. Roberts
Foundation, Dallas.

Published by the Texas State Historical Association in cooperation with the Center
for Studies in Texas History at the University of Texas at Austin.

Cover: *Battle of Palo Alto* (detail) by Carl Nebel. Hand-colored lithograph, $11\frac{1}{16}$ x
$16\frac{11}{16}$ in. (composition), from Carl Nebel and George Wilkins Kendall, *The War
Between the United States and Mexico Illustrated* (New York: D. Appleton, 1851).
Courtesy the DeGolyer Library, Southern Methodist University, Dallas.

Texas and the Mexican War

A History and a Guide

By Charles M. Robinson III

Texas State
Historical Association

CONTENTS

ACKNOWLEDGMENTS

I WISH TO EXPRESS MY appreciation to several individuals and institutions for their help and encouragement in this project, inlcuding Thomas Carroll (retired), Aaron Mahr-Yáñez, and Douglas Murphy of the National Park Service; Walter Plitt III of Brownsville, Texas; Ingewall Hansen of San Benito, Texas; Ron Tyler, Holly Taylor, and George Ward (retired) of the Texas State Historical Assocation; Manuel Hinojosa of Port Isabel, Texas; Texas State Library and Archives, Austin; Center for American History, University of Texas at Austin; and the Library of Congress and National Archives in Washington, D.C.

Thanks also to the following for permission to reprint extracts from published works:

Courtesy of Gerald Barry Hurst, Jacksonville, N.C.: James Buckner Barry, *Buck Barry, Texas Ranger and Frontiersman* (Bison Books ed.; Lincoln: University of Nebraska Press, 1984).

Courtesy of University of North Texas Press, Denton: James M. McCaffrey (ed.), *"Surrounded by Dangers of All Kinds": The Mexican War Letters of Lieutenant Theodore Laidley* (Denton: University of North Texas Press, 1997).

Courtesy of the University of Texas Press, Austin: John Salmon Ford, *Rip Ford's Texas*, ed. Stephen B. Oates (Austin: University of Texas Press, 1963; reprint,1994).

Courtesy of TCU Press, Fort Worth: Joseph E. Chance (ed.), *Mexico Under Fire: Being the Diary of Samuel Ryan Curtis, 3rd Ohio Volunteer Regiment, During the American Military Occupation of*

Northern Mexico, 1846–1847 (Fort Worth: Texas Christian University Press, 1994).

Courtesy of Texas Western Press, University of Texas at El Paso: Lawrence Clayton and Joseph E. Chance (eds.), *The March to Monterrey: The Diary of Lt. Rankin Dilworth* (El Paso: Texas Western Press, 1996).

Charles M. Robinson III

1.
TEXAS, MANIFEST DESTINY, AND NATIONAL HONOR

THE UNITED STATES FOUGHT a war with Mexico for several reasons: annexation of Texas to the United States, the American belief in Manifest Destiny, political instability in Mexico, and a desire for war in both countries. The last reason is perhaps the most important and, in our time, the most overlooked. The current opinion, which arose even as the war was entering its final phases and has been accepted ever since, was that the United States, a great power, arbitrarily provoked a war with Mexico, a weak power, for territorial aggrandizement.

The idea took hold in Mexico as military disasters followed one another in rapid succession, culminating in the loss of almost half its territory. The situation was further aggravated by the generally condescending attitude of the United States government toward Mexico in the years since the war and by what Mexicans perceive as various and routine U.S. infringements on their national sovereignty.

In the United States, there are several causes for the view that the war was unprovoked and unpopular. Although the antiwar Whig Party was entering the final decade of its existence as the war ended, the American press still was largely Whig controlled. Whig authors, such as Nathaniel Covington Brooks with his exhaustive and appropriately titled *Complete History of the Mexican War*, and Col. Albert C. Ramsey of the Eleventh Infantry, who translated, edited, and annotated a compilation prepared by a group of Mexican participants in the war, appear to have been more numerous than expansionist authors like John Stilwell Jenkins, whose equally competent *History of the War between the United States and Mexico* appeared almost simultaneously with Brooks's work.[1] The claim of Whig politicians that the war was nothing more than a Southern conspiracy to create a slave empire in the West seemed validated with the free soil controversies that arose during the following decade, culminating in the Civil War.[2] The fact that future notables like Abraham Lincoln and Ulysses S. Grant opposed the Mexican War also lent credence to a modern view of the war as an act of aggression, and in the 1960s and 1970s it became fashionable to compare the Mexican War with the ongoing conflicts in Vietnam and Cambodia. Finally, one must not overlook the fact that, in terms of deaths against the number of troops in the field, it was the costliest war in U.S. history. As the casualty lists grew, so did opposition to the war.

But the facts as viewed in 1845 and early 1846 were far different. In territory, Mexico approached the size of the United States (neither country had clearly defined boundaries with the other, and the boundary between the United States and the British possessions to the north was in dispute). In the spring of 1846 the Mexican army was at least twice the size of its U.S. counterpart. It also was more battle-seasoned, having been used to suppress (and often create) insurrections against the national government. The army had suffered a few setbacks; it had been defeated in Texas and was unable to quell the defiance of the great families that ruled Upper California. These provinces, however, were too distant for the military supply system in Mexico, and Texas was conveniently located near major sources of manpower and equipment from the United States. The army remained a major factor of Mexican political development, albeit one frequently on the verge of mutiny.[3]

Outwardly, no two countries could be more dissimilar. Even with the growing sectionalism that eventually led to four years of devastating civil war, the United States had a remarkably stable government that changed by election at fixed intervals according to constitutional means. Mexico, on the other hand, could hardly be said to have a government at all. Its first fifty years of national existence were cursed by coups d'etat that sapped its energy and resources.

Outward appearances are deceiving, however. The political situation in both countries demanded war. Both were new, only recently having broken away from foreign rule. The United States, which achieved independence from Great Britain in the 1780s, was compelled to fight the British again from 1812 to 1815 to attain true respect as a sovereign power. Mexico spent its first twenty years of independence from Spain fending off incursions by European nations. Both the United States and Mexico emerged from these struggles with a xenophobic nationalism that distrusted anything different or foreign. This nationalism quickly developed into national paranoia.

When the ascendancy of the liberal reformers in Spain removed that threat, Mexico turned her nationalist fears to the north. In the 1820s, first Spain, then Mexico, had allowed American colonization of Texas as a buffer against United States expansion. Much of the province was empty because, in three hundred years, neither Spaniard nor Mexican had shown any particular interest in living there. Within the first seven years of colonization, however, Americans had come in such numbers and been so successful that they had all but overwhelmed the local Mexican population. Mexican efforts to restrict this growth and suppress the English-speaking population ultimately led the Texans to armed rebellion and the establishment of an independent republic. The rebellion had been openly supported in the United States, which to the Mexicans was conclusive evidence of a long-suspected American plot to dismember their country.[5]

In the United States, the removal of the immediate British threat brought an overabundance of national self-confidence. American politicians, reflecting and in some cases manipulating the public attitudes of the day, adopted an evangelical attitude that viewed their nation and institutions as the hope of the world. But in order to make converts, evangelists must have enemies; if political evangelists have no enemies, they must be created. In the case of the United States, it was Europe.

As with Mexico, one U.S. quarrel involved Spain. The Louisiana Purchase had grown in the American imagination until it included Texas, under the very dubious notion that La Salle's ill-fated seventeenth-century shadow colony gave France sovereignty in the nineteenth century. This was thought to have been settled in 1819, when a treaty fixed the boundary between American Louisiana and Spanish Texas at the Sabine River. But the United States never completely abandoned the belief that it held lawful title to Texas, which became a preoccupation with various U.S. administrations, both Democratic and Whig, despite the latter party's subsequent claims to the contrary.[6]

Ironically, the first attempt to obtain Texas for the United States was made in 1825 by a Whig president, the same man who only six years earlier had negotiated the treaty recognizing Spanish sovereignty—John Quincy Adams. Adams's action reflected the prevailing American view throughout the first half of the nineteenth century, that Mexicans were incapable of self-government. The logical extension of that view was that Mexico likewise was incapable of developing, or even appreciating, the vast potential of its northern provinces, and that it would be better for all concerned, including Mexico, if they came under U.S. rule. Adams's successor, Andrew Jackson, was even more adamant. He firmly believed that Texas rightfully belonged to the United States under the Louisiana Purchase, had been illegally surrendered to Spain/Mexico, and should be brought back into the fold. The establishment of the Republic of Texas near the end of Jackson's administration only whetted American ambitions. By the same token, Spain and subsequently Mexico viewed the Louisiana claims as "palpable absurdities."[7]

The prime American fear, however, remained Great Britain. Despite the War of 1812, a suspicion of British imperial goals remained in the recesses of the national mentality. A boundary dispute with the British over the Oregon territory and growing diplomatic ties between the new Republic of Texas and the European powers ignited a baseless, but very real, fear of encirclement. The

British already had Canada. Might they not also grab Oregon and California and establish a protectorate in Texas? It therefore became necessary for the United States to strike first—to fulfill what many believed was the country's "Manifest Destiny" to expand its institutions throughout the continent to the benefit of those (i.e., Mexicans and American Indians) who were not so enlightened. Most American politicians aspiring to national office echoed this sentiment.[8] If the nation were to reach outward, however, it would be at the expense of Mexico. Consequently, as one contemporary author noted, expansionists saw the Mexican War as "the opening of a new volume of American history."[9]

In Mexico, meanwhile, the government shifted back and forth between various blocs. The Federalist faction, as the name implies, wanted a federated republic with much of the power invested in the states. The conservative Centralists, on the other hand, wanted a supreme national government upholding the privileges of Mexico's small ruling class and operating in close association with the Roman Catholic Church. The Federalists themselves were divided into the moderates, who sought to accept the reality of Texas's independence and accommodation with the United States, and the *puros*, or purists, an extreme group that opposed any concessions to the north. The Centralists were divided among conservatives, monarchists, and the clerical faction. Playing every faction against the others were the Santanistas, opportunistic supporters of the oft-deposed, but invariably reinstated, dictator Antonio López de Santa Anna.

A complete view of the complex series of events that led to war is beyond the scope of this work. Of immediate concern is the annexation of Texas, finalized in 1845, which prompted Mexico to break off diplomatic relations and go on a war footing. When Mexican moderates suggested recognizing the political realities, they drew almost universal opposition from the other factions, as well as the army, the public, and the press. Each group accused its enemies of betraying the nation by seeking reconciliation with the United States. In the face of public outcry throughout Mexico, even those who previously had supported the moderate position now considered war the only viable alternative. Although the moderate

José Joaquín Herrera was elected president in September 1845, a much larger coalition was prepared to accept war and possible defeat rather than compromise. As in the United States, any Mexican politician who proposed sacrificing national honor in the face of reality did so at his peril. This position would cost Mexico dearly in the long run.[10]

The previous March, James K. Polk had assumed the presidency of the United States. President Polk's initial goal was to complete the process of annexing Texas, begun under his predecessor, John Tyler, and he hoped to do it without bloodshed. He likewise hoped to acquire the western part of New Mexico, which at that time included Arizona as well as northern California.[11] To that end, Polk appointed John Slidell minister plenipotentiary to Mexico to negotiate a Texas boundary settlement with a border along the entire Rio Grande and the purchase of California and New Mexico west of the Rio Grande. Believing the region vital to the nation, Polk considered the potential cost to be "of small importance." He thought he could get it for $15 or $20 million but was prepared to go as high as $40 million if necessary.

Slidell arrived in Veracruz on November 30, 1845, to the surprise of the Herrera government, which did not believe an envoy would be appointed until after the U.S. Congress convened on December 1. Politically, Herrera was too weak to establish any sort of mandate or consensus, and the fact that Slidell was even allowed to land was viewed as treason in many circles. In San Luis Potosí, north of Mexico City, the commander of the Army of the North, Maj. Gen. Mariano Paredes y Arrillaga, opposed any effort at reconciliation, and on December 14 he declared against the government. His stand, while self-serving, drew widespread support even among the *puros* of Herrera's own party, and on December 30, 1845, the Herrera government fell. Three days later Paredes assumed the presidency. Although Slidell remained in Mexico a few more months, Polk and his advisors had totally underestimated the sense of outrage among the Mexican people. If the United States meant to have Texas, it would have to fight.[12]

The Mexicans' enthusiasm was matched by the average citizens of the United States. Despite later Whig arguments about slavery and aggrandizement, many shared Polk's view that expansion into new territory would scatter the population and dilute any potential for centralized, and thereby abusive, political and economic power. Once war began, the ease with which the United States was able to field an army of volunteers to support its regular troops demonstrated the exhilaration of the day. Even those tempted to question Polk's justification were prone to accept his explanation for the war and initially supported his position, although they later turned against it. The fourteen northern Whigs of the House of Representatives who voted against the declaration of war ultimately came to be called the "Immortal Fourteen," but in the beginning they were vilified, particularly in western states like Ohio and Illinois.[13]

The popularity of Mexican War memoirs until the eve of the Civil War illustrated pride in the achievement. So did Polk's triumphant tour of the supposedly antiwar New England states in the summer of 1847, as the conflict entered its second year. So did the tendency to name or rename towns and counties after Mexican War victories, resulting in countless Cerro Gordos, Palo Altos, and Buena Vistas.[14] Given the popular mood in both countries, war became inevitable.

Gen. Zachary Taylor's camp at Corpus Christi appears placid in this view, belying the months of boredom, rattlesnakes, and generally miserable living conditions as the men waited out events in Washington and Mexico City. *John Frost,* Pictorial History of Mexico and the Mexican War *(Philadelphia: Charles Desilver, 1862), Author's Collection.*

2.
"HOSTILITIES . . . HAVE BEEN COMMENCED"

SOON AFTER TAKING OFFICE IN MARCH 1845, President Polk ordered Bvt. Brig. Gen. Zachary Taylor to assemble two thousand troops at Fort Jesup, Louisiana, on the presumption that Texas would agree to the annexation terms recently approved by the U.S. Congress. On May 28, Secretary of War William L. Marcy advised Taylor that as soon as the Texas Congress consented to annexation and convened an assembly to accept the U.S. terms, the government in Washington would consider it entitled to U.S. protection "from foreign invasion and Indian incursions." In the event of Indian depredations, Taylor was instructed to consult with Texas authorities because of their "superior local knowledge," but would not serve under their jurisdiction.

The possibility of an invasion "by a foreign power" (specifically Mexico) was far more ticklish, because Texas itself would remain a foreign nation until formal U.S. jurisdiction was established. In that case, Marcy told Taylor to immediately deploy his forces according to his own judgment, but indicated he should do so only "after her convention shall have acceded to the terms of annexation."[1]

The sixty-year-old Taylor was a veteran of the War of 1812, where he had been the first U.S. soldier ever to earn a brevet promotion. He also had served in numerous Indian conflicts, developing into a tough, no-nonsense soldier with little regard for hierarchy or for military polish and ceremony. "In dress he was

THEN AND NOW

To follow Taylor's route from the very beginning, the best place to start is Fort Jesup State Commemorative Area, six miles east of Many, Louisiana, on Louisiana Highway 6. The highway itself formerly was known as the San Antonio Road, because it connected San Antonio with Natchitoches, Louisiana. Although the fort once had eighty-two structures, the only original building is an old kitchen/mess hall restored to its original appearance. An officer's house has been reconstructed as a museum, and locations of other structures are marked. Ironically, the annexation of Texas and the subsequent Mexican War negated the need for frontier defense in Louisiana, and Fort Jesup was abandoned in 1846.

In Corpus Christi, the exact site of Fort Marcy is not known, but it is safe to say it is largely covered by the downtown area. Artesian Park, 800 Chaparral Street, contains a granite monument to Taylor erected by the Daughters of the American Revolution. Nearby is a state historical marker erected in 1976. Old Bayview Cemetery at Ramirez and Padre Streets contains the graves of seven soldiers who were killed when the steamboat Dayton exploded shortly after noon on September 12, 1845. The burial site was selected by Lt. Col. Ethan Allen Hitchcock.

possibly too plain, rarely wearing anything in the field to indicate his rank, or even that he was an officer," 2d Lt. Ulysses S. Grant, Fourth Infantry, recalled. But he added that Taylor "was known to every soldier in his army, and was respected by all." Sloppy and overweight, Taylor was nonetheless an outstanding field commander and the first choice of presidents in times of potential crisis. With the possibility of a confrontation with Mexico over annexation, he was the logical choice.[2]

On July 4 the Texas convention assembled in Austin and accepted the United States' terms. Texas would formally enter the United States the following February. Taylor was ordered to take up a position along the Gulf, enforcing the boundary Texas and the United States claimed along the Rio Grande. Aware of Mexico's contention that the Nueces was the southwestern boundary of Texas, Polk and Marcy were adamant that he avoid "all aggressive measures towards Mexico, as long as the relations of

Gen. Zachary Taylor was an easygoing commander with a dry, highly developed sense of humor and little patience for military decorum. In battle, he preferred giving his unit commanders a set of objectives he expected and leaving it to their discretion to carry them out according to the circumstances they might encounter. Nevertheless, Taylor was a tough, tenacious fighter who would hold on, even when the odds were against him. *Prints and Photographs Division, Library of Congress, Washington, D.C.*

peace exist between that republic and the United States." Consequently, he was cautioned not to molest any posts garrisoned by Mexican troops in the disputed area, nor to occupy any Mexican towns over which Texas did not exercise actual jurisdiction. His primary duty was to block any hostile move Mexico might make during Texas's final months as a sovereign nation. At the behest of Andrew Jackson Donelson, U.S. chargé d'affaires in Texas, Taylor also agreed to send the Second Dragoons overland to San Antonio, although this probably was as much to spare their horses the rigors of a sea voyage as it was to satisfy Donelson's desire for a show of force in the interior.

The first of Taylor's troops embarked from New Orleans for the Nueces on July 22. Taylor himself arrived at Aransas Pass with eight companies of infantry three days later. It soon became obvious that heavy shoaling in the coastal waters would hinder any efforts to land troops and supply a base at the mouth of the Nueces, so eventually he opted to establish his depot at Corpus Christi, where troops began a defensive work designated as Fort Marcy.[3]

Ranger captain Jack Hays was an experienced frontiersman, whose reputation prompted Taylor to invite him to organize a campany of scouts to observe Mexican movements. *Author's Collection.*

Taylor's efforts essentially were a U.S. military operation, but the question remained as to where Texas would fit into the plan. It was, after all, still an independent nation, and the American troops technically were a foreign occupation force. The War Department instructed Taylor to arrange with the Texas government for the enlistment of local troops. Although Texas President Anson Jones wanted U.S. troops to establish a garrison in Austin to defend the frontier, Taylor rejected the idea. While not as alarmed as his superiors about rumors of growing Mexican militancy, he nevertheless believed that war was likely, and he did not want his forces divided. Instead, he passed on the War Department's recommendation that Texas's existing "volunteers or spies" (by which he meant the Texas Rangers) be mustered into U.S. service, adding that he would recommend they continue to receive the same pay from the United States that they had drawn from Texas.[4]

Taylor would have no trouble convincing the Texans to enlist, because John C. "Captain Jack" Hays, one of the most prominent Ranger commanders, wrote from San Antonio offering to organize a company of mounted volunteers. Already impressed by Hays's reputation, Taylor replied that he could serve as major of a Ranger company that would be mustered into service under U.S. militia regulations. Their duty would be "procuring intelligence of the movements of the Mexicans and protecting the Frontier against Indian Depredations." Hays was cautioned, however, not to disturb "any Mexican Establishment on this side [of] the Rio Grande unless it be rendered necessary by an attack or demonstration," not to disturb Mexican settlements, and not to provoke hostilities.[5]

This was easier said than done. The love-hate relationship between Texans and Mexicans ran deep. On the one hand, U.S. officers at Corpus Christi, aware of the old animosities, were amazed at the amicable trade relations that, throughout the existence of the republic, had been a vital part of its economy. On the other hand, many Rangers had bitter memories of Mexican imprisonment following the ill-fated Mier and Santa Fe expeditions, or had other reasons for hating Mexico. These feelings were noted by Grant, who wrote, "The hostilities between Texans and Mexicans was [sic] so great that neither was safe in the neighborhood of the other."[6]

The animosity did not concern Taylor, who seemed mainly interested in using Rangers as defense against the Indians, leaving U.S. troops free to deal with Mexico. They would be enlisted for three months, and, if tensions with Mexico eased, they could be discharged by the end of the year. Two companies were mustered into service in late September, the first in Victoria and Goliad under Capt. John T. Price, and the second in San Antonio under Capt. Addison Gillespie. But with little trouble on the frontier, and Taylor not requiring their services in Corpus Christi, they mainly hung around their respective areas waiting for something to do. They had little doubt, however, that trouble with Mexico ultimately would erupt, and they prepared accordingly. Knives received special attention. They knew that the *rancheros*, their Mexican counterparts, were specialists in lariating—roping a man around the neck, jerking him off his horse, and dragging him to death. They intended to be ready.[7]

The U.S. troops, meanwhile, had adjusted to their surroundings on the Texas coast, and many found the semitropical region pleasant. The temperature was a welcome change from the north, and a

Soldiers designated as cooks prepare a chicken and a pig for their company's mess. The Texans were especially adept at making off with local livestock. *John Frost, Pictorial History of Mexico and the Mexican War (Philadelphia: Charles Desilver, 1862), Author's Collection.*

constant breeze from the Gulf of Mexico moderated the midday heat. "We live first rate here," one soldier wrote to his family in Massachusetts, "plenty of beef and mutton, occasionally venison and fish in any quantity. There is a seine belonging to the regiment, and a party go out every day to supply the regiment. I have seen fifty or sixty bushels brought in at one time, each fish weighing from two to ten pounds, some averaging about twelve or fifteen."[8]

There were some drawbacks. "Every tree and bush has its thorn," one officer noted, adding, "Our camp-ground is infested with rattle-snakes; as many as two at a time have been found in the tents of the officers." The breeze that kept the camp cool also could blow in heavy gusts that threatened to knock down the tents.[9]

The pleasant weather gave way to the cold, windy, overcast Texas winter. Tents were inadequate, blankets were in short supply, and the troops grew miserable and restless. Sutlers charged exorbitant prices for basic commodities like potatoes and onions, and drinking water was scarce and brackish. Soldiers suffered from cold, damp, and dysentery. Camp followers abounded, and by November the population of Corpus Christi had reached a thousand. Liquor was plentiful. Soldiers became drunk and committed outrages against the local Mexican population, prompting Taylor to restrict the entire army to camp at night. Officers quarreled over rank and position. To provide some amusement, a group of officers, led by Capt. John B. Magruder, First Artillery, contributed to build a theater where they themselves would perform, hoping to recoup their investment at the box office. The venture was so successful that ultimately professional troupes were booked to follow the army into Mexico.[10]

Relief came when, on January 13, Secretary of War Marcy passed on President Polk's order that Taylor was to advance to the Rio Grande (which Marcy called the Rio del Norte) and occupy the east bank. Again, he was to do nothing to provoke Mexico. If, however, Mexico declared war or showed any other acts of hostility, he was to act "not . . . merely on the defensive, if your relative means enable you to do otherwise." In other words, the operations, once war broke out, would be entirely at Taylor's discretion.[11]

This was welcome news to Taylor, who was eager to get his army on the move. It was essential to secure a harbor near the Rio Grande to ensure that his forces could be supplied directly from New Orleans, and the best option appeared to be Point Isabel, which served as the port for Matamoros. It was on a bay sheltered by Padre Island with access through Brazos Santiago Pass. He had been assured cooperation from Cmdre. David Conner, commander of the naval squadron operating in the gulf, and after considering two lines of march, one along the mainland and one down Padre Island, he opted for the mainland. He believed the mere presence of the U.S. Army on the Rio Grande would "produce a powerful effect" in keeping Mexico quiet. "From the best information I am able to obtain, and which I deem as authentic as any," Taylor advised the War Department, "I do not believe that our advance to the banks of the Rio Grande will be resisted. The army, however, will go fully prepared for a state of hostilities, should they unfortunately be provoked by the Mexicans."[12]

On February 19, 1846, President Jones relinquished executive power to J. Pinckney Henderson, governor of the new state of Texas, which now was an integral part of the United States. Taylor, meanwhile, prepared for his march south along the Arroyo Colorado Road that ran from the Nueces to Matamoros. He sent two companies to establish a depot on Santa Gertrudis Creek, forty miles west of Corpus Christi, with four days forage for animals and subsistence for troops. Maj. John Munroe was to travel by sea from Corpus Christi to Brazos Santiago with a siege train, a battery of artillery, engineers, quartermasters, ordnance, and pay departments timed to arrive when the army was in the vicinity of Point Isabel. The army now consisted of about 3,550 officers and men, with a train of 307 carts and wagons. On March 8, as the first units of cavalry and light artillery marched out, Taylor issued a general order in English and Spanish, for circulation in Matamoros, Mier, and Camargo on the Rio Grande.[13]

Head-quarters, Army of Occupation
Corpus Christi, March 8, 1846
Order No. 30

The army of occupation of Texas being now about to take a position upon the left bank of the Rio Grande, under the orders of the Executive of the United States, the general-in-chief desires to express the hope that the movement will be advantageous to all concerned; and with the object of attaining this laudable end, he has ordered all under his command to observe, with the most scrupulous respect, the rights of all the inhabitants who may be found in peaceful prosecution of their respective occupations, as well on the left as on the right side of the Rio Grande. Under no pretext, nor in any way, will any interference be allowed with the civil rights or religious privileges of the inhabitants, but the utmost respect for them will be maintained.

Whatsoever may be needed for the use of the army will be bought by the proper purveyor, and paid for at the highest prices. The general-in-chief has the satisfaction to say that he confides in the patriotism and discipline of the army under his command, and that he feels sure that his orders will be obeyed with the utmost exactness.

Z. Taylor,
Brevet Brig. Gen. U.S.A., commanding[14]

THEN AND NOW

Taylor's march from Corpus Christi to the Rio Grande approximately follows U.S. 77 south as far as Raymondville. A historical marker on Business 77 about a quarter of a mile south of General Cavazos Boulevard in Kingsville indicates the site of Taylor's depot on Santa Gertrudis Creek. Another marker at a roadside park on U.S. 77 between Kingsville and Riviera describes the march. The Department of Highways and Public Transportation's rest stop on U.S. 77 in Kenedy County marks a campsite.

Paso Real, the ford where the army crossed the Arroyo Colorado, is commemorated by a state historical marker at the intersection of FM 508 and FM 1420 about a mile east of Rio Hondo. The marker, however, dwells on the ferry that served stagecoaches and makes no mention of the Mexican War. The ford itself, about ten miles east of the marker, has been dredged away to create a barge channel.

The instructions regarding religious liberty were two-edged. On the one hand, they were intended to assure the almost exclusively Roman Catholic Mexicans that their religion would be respected, and on the other, to rein in potential trouble among overly enthusiastic Protestant U.S. soldiers. Nativism and anti-Catholicism were rampant in the United States at the time, and native Protestant mobs had rioted in several large American cities. Within the army, foreign-born and Roman Catholic soldiers frequently were subjected to harassment.[15]

Whatever the prejudices, most were glad to be on the march. "We are off for the Rio Grande!" an elated Capt. W. S. Henry of the Third Infantry wrote in his diary. In an awkwardly spelled letter to his fiancée, Julia Dent, Grant wrote:

It is believed by many [that the Mexicans] will make us fight for our ground before we will be allowed to occupy it. But fight or no fight evry one rejoises at the idea of leaving Corpus Christi. It is to be hoped that our troops being so close on the borders of Mexico will bring about a speedy settlement of the boundary question.[16]

This latest move only reinforced Mexico's belief in American perfidy. While Polk and Slidell professed peace, Conner's warships

Looking more like Captain Cook's landing in Tahiti, a fanciful illustration shows troops being rowed ashore at Point Isabel from large ships. In reality the larger ships could not clear the bar and anchored off Brazos Santiago. *John Frost,* Pictorial History of Mexico and the Mexican War *(Philadelphia: Charles Desilver, 1862), Author's Collection.*

cruised the Mexican Gulf Coast, and a second U.S. squadron hovered off California. Now Taylor was moving south. "Whom did they hope to deceive with such false appearances?" a contemporary Mexican writer asked. Whether Texas was a province in rebellion, a sovereign republic, or a part of the United States, Mexico considered its southern boundary to be the Nueces River, not the Rio Grande. This had been the historic boundary, first under Spanish, then under Mexican jurisdiction. Therefore, and regardless of any other considerations, Taylor's entry into the no-man's-land between the two rivers, which Polk saw as the lawful occupation of home territory, was viewed by Mexico (and increasingly by Polk's opponents in the United States) as an invasion.[17]

The Mexicans had already used more than diplomacy to express their resentment. One incident involved the American schooner *Susannah*, which had left New Orleans for Corpus Christi on November 13 and was caught in a storm. Damaged

A more realistic view of Point Isabel shows a few buildings clustered on bleak bluffs, with only small boats in the bay. *John Frost,* Pictorial History of Mexico and the Mexican War *(Philadelphia: Charles Desilver, 1862), Author's Collection.*

and leaking, she put into the Port of Matamoros "in distress" for repairs and reprovisioning. Instead of assisting in conformance with trade agreements between the United States and Mexico, Mexican customs officials seized the ship on the grounds that Corpus Christi, the declared destination, was "a Mexican port, not open to foreign commerce." The *Susannah* was taken up the river to Matamoros, where all her tackle was stripped for Mexican government use. Her master, Samuel H. Clay, was fined double the value of the cargo and imprisoned until December 22, when he was released on bond but ordered to remain in the city. On March 1, his bond was revoked, and he was jailed until April 15, 1846, when he was sent under heavy guard to San Fernando, ninety miles to the south.[18]

Meanwhile, on March 19, the Second Dragoons, sent ahead to reconnoiter, reached the ford of the Arroyo Colorado, a little more than thirty miles north of Matamoros, where they were challenged by Mexican *rancheros* on the opposite bank. Although the Mexicans did not offer a fight, they made it clear that any attempt to cross would be considered a hostile act. Given this information, Taylor prepared to fight his way across, and early the following morning he positioned his infantry and cavalry at the ford, with artillery ready to sweep the opposite bank. The Mexicans reappeared, and one officer crossed to advise Taylor that any attempt to ford the arroyo would be considered an act of war. He also handed Taylor a broadside issued by Maj. Gen. Francisco Mejía, commander of the Mexican forces assembled at Matamoros.[19] Its tone left no doubt about the Mexican position.

Until the long wished for day shall arrive, when we enter upon the great campaign for the re-conquest of the territory of which we have been despoiled [i.e., Texas], and to carry our eagles in triumph to the banks of the Sabine, we, who have the glory to be in front of the invaders, must serve as an impenetrable barrier. . . .

Soldiers: The hour of danger is come; you know your duty, and will fulfill it with honor and patriotism. . . . Let the enemy then come, whom you are burning to meet on the field of battle.[20]

Ignoring the Mexican protests, Taylor began crossing his troops. The Mexicans withdrew in the direction of Matamoros, and he allowed them to depart. Nevertheless, it was the first indication of open hostility by the Mexicans, and he thought it significant enough to make a detailed report to Washington.

On the night of March 23, a Mexican arrived from Point Isabel with news that the troops guarding the port had burned the buildings and retreated toward Matamoros. Taylor dispatched Bvt. Brig. Gen. William Jenkins Worth with the infantry to occupy a suitable location on the Rio Grande opposite Matamoros, while he took the cavalry and his empty wagons to secure Point Isabel. An advance unit of cavalry was sent ahead and managed to bring the fires under control with the loss of only a few houses. Most of the people had fled toward Matamoros. Taylor's arrival coincided with that of the steamers, and soon supplies were being lightered ashore. The engineers set to work laying out earthen fortifications. Two companies of artillery under Bvt. Maj. John Munroe were detached to form the garrison. "Our great depot must be here," Taylor reported, "and it is very important to secure it against any enterprise of the enemy."[21]

Brig. Gen. William Jenkins Worth impressed his Mexican counterparts by his military bearing. *Library of Congress.*

Now that he had established his base, Taylor and the dragoons rejoined the main force on the plain at Palo Alto, about ten miles north of Matamoros. From there the army marched on to the Rio Grande, reaching it about 11 A.M., March 28. Taylor went into camp just opposite Matamoros, and within a short time a flagstaff had been erected and the U.S. flag run up. Now the soldiers could see a Mexican city for the first time, and Grant sent his impressions to Julia: "The city from this side of the river bears a very imposing appearance and no doubt contains from four to five thousand inhabitants," he noted. Although the Mexicans had erected breastworks and mounted a cannon facing the American camp, he doubted they meant anything by it. "Already they have boasted and threatened so much and executed so little that it is generally believed that all they are doing is mere bombast and show, intended to intimidate our troops."[22]

Taylor ordered General Worth across the river with a letter assuring General Mejía of the Americans' peaceful intentions. Mejía, however, sent his second-in-command, Brig. Gen. Romulo Díaz de la Vega, who met Worth under a tree on the riverbank. Although protocol was on Mejia's side (he was, after all, Taylor's equal and not obligated to meet a subordinate), Worth was offended and refused to deliver Taylor's letter. Instead, he read it. Díaz de la Vega politely listened to the translation, then gave Mexico's position that the U.S. forces were illegally occupying Mexican territory. When Worth demanded to see the U.S. consul, the Mexican officer replied that the demand would be referred to General Mejía. Now thoroughly irritated, Worth said the refusal would be deemed a belligerent act. He also told Díaz de la Vega that if any armed party of Mexicans crossed the river, it would be regarded as an act of war. With that, the meeting broke up.[23]

Meanwhile, two dragoons, who for some reason were separated from the main body, were captured and carried to Matamoros as prisoners. "This seizure caused no little excitement, and we were all ready to take the city at any risk," Captain Henry remarked. Taylor, however, was less excitable and initially suspected that they might have been deserters. Although in this case he was mistaken (the two, in fact, were prisoners and subsequently were returned by General Mejía), desertion quickly became a problem. Almost immediately upon Taylor's arrival at the river, the Mexicans had begun efforts to entice U.S. soldiers to desert and to some extent had been successful. Within the first week, four deserters drowned while trying to swim the river, and two were killed by pickets. Although much has been made about a contingent of deserters that later formed the San Patricio Battalion of the Mexican army, Taylor noted that most of the deserters were "old offenders," often native-born malcontents, together with some recruits whose sense of personal freedom was affronted by the discipline of a professional army. By April 11 the Mexicans were claiming that some forty-three soldiers and six slaves had deserted to their side of the river, and on April 20 they announced a grant of 320 acres of land to any deserter who would take out Mexican citizenship.[24]

The return of the two dragoons on the one hand, and the encouragement of desertion on the other, indicated the extent of growing uncertainties and the overall deterioration of relations. On April 8 the troops broke ground for a fieldwork across from Matamoros. The earthen fort was designed as a hexagon, with bastions at each corner, and bombproof shelters, the whole surrounded by a ditch. Taylor referred to it variously as "Fort Texas" and "Camp near Matamoras." Two days later, Col. Truman Cross,

THEN AND NOW

The site of the fortifications at Point Isabel includes the general area of Point Isabel Lighthouse State Park between Maxan Street and Highway 100 near the foot of the Queen Isabella Causeway in Port Isabel. The earthwork fortifications, which Taylor later designated Fort Polk, survived into the twentieth century. In the 1920s, however, developers of Port Isabel leveled them as part of a general grading and cutting down of the bluffs overlooking the Laguna Madre. The only remnant is the mound topped by the lighthouse, which was erected on the bastion point. There is a state historical marker for Fort Polk on the lighthouse grounds. A second state marker, noting the area's significance as the Port of Matamoros, is a block away at the foot of Maxan Street fronting the Laguna Madre. The Port Isabel Historical Museum, at the intersection of Railroad and Tarnava Streets, occupies the Champion Building, which, after the lighthouse, is the oldest structure in town. It has a highly developed Mexican War exhibit, including artifacts recovered in Port Isabel, at Camp Belknap, Palo Alto Battlefield, and Buena Vista Battlefield.

chief quartermaster, wandered away from camp and did not return. Several search parties were sent out to look for him, and Taylor ordered guns to be fired to help guide him back to camp. When he did not return, Henry wrote in his diary, "I fear he is either a prisoner, or has been murdered."[25]

While the troops wondered about Cross, bells and an artillery salute announced the arrival in Matamoros of Maj. Gen. Pedro de Ampudia, commander of the Division of the North, to replace the vacillating and ineffectual General Mejía. Ampudia arrived from Monterrey with a 200-man cavalry escort, but the bulk of his force, 2,200 men under Brig. Gen. Anastacio Torrejón, was expected within three days. One of his first acts was to dispatch a note to Taylor accusing the United States of belligerent acts, which the Mexican government was no longer willing to tolerate. Consequently, he demanded that Taylor break camp and begin withdrawing to the Nueces within twenty-four hours. Otherwise, Ampudia said, "I advise you that we accept the war to which, with so much injustice on your part, you provoke us."[26]

The Mexican officers delivering Ampudia's note remained in the U.S. camp only a few minutes. A short time later, some officers were warming themselves by the fire when Capt. William W. S. Bliss, Taylor's son-in-law and adjutant, rode by and said, "Well, you may get ready; it's coming." The camp was reorganized to withstand a bombardment, and labor on the defense work was hurried forward. The following morning, Taylor sent a reply to Ampudia, stating that he intended to remain in place and warning the Mexicans against opening fire.[27]

Amid the growing tensions, the Americans continued to fret about the disappearance of Colonel Cross, and it was now generally assumed that he was dead. Two search parties went out. One returned without incident, but the other, under Lt. Theodoric H. Porter, Fourth Infantry, was ambushed and badly mauled by a band of Mexican irregulars. A soldier named Flood was killed, and Porter was surrounded and hacked to death. Two separate squads were sent out to recover the bodies, but the U.S. troops were so ignorant of the terrain that they could not even locate the scene of the fight. Two days later, on April 21, a Mexican came into camp saying that he knew the location of the body of an American officer. A detachment was immediately dispatched and identified the body as Cross. There was a hole in his skull where he apparently had been clubbed. There was no question that he, like Porter, had been killed by irregulars.[28]

Taylor, however, now had his own irregular troops who understood *ranchero* tactics and fought in kind. These were seventy-seven Texas Rangers under Capt. Samuel Walker, who had arrived in Point Isabel in mid-April. Reporting to Major Monroe, they were ordered to gather intelligence and establish communications between the depot at Point Isabel and Taylor's camp on the Rio Grande. The Rangers were formally mustered into federal service on April 21. Although Taylor considered them undisciplined rabble, their knowledge of the country made them invaluable as scouts and couriers.[29]

However useful seventy-seven Rangers might be, Taylor faced a much greater problem across the Rio Grande, where General Torrejón had arrived in Matamoros with the main Mexican force.

Ampudia now was ready to cross the Rio Grande and expel the U.S. forces. He postponed the operation, though, because of yet another change in command. Ampudia might have been more decisive than Mejía, but as a commander, he was only marginally competent. His reputation for wanton cruelty, and the fact that he was Cuban rather than Mexican, made him generally detested by the army. His successor was the forty-two-year-old Maj. Gen. Mariano Arista, who formerly had commanded the Division of the North, but had been removed because of his lukewarm enthusiasm for the Paredes administration. Even so, he was capable. The troops and public had confidence in him, and, bowing to public pressure in the northern states, Paredes reinstated him. Arista had an additional advantage; he had lived briefly in Cincinnati, and although his knowledge of the United States was far from extensive, it nevertheless was superior to that of most other Mexican officers. His arrival on April 24, at the head of more troops, brought the Mexican strength in Matamoros up to approximately five thousand. Ampudia remained as second in command.[30]

The day of Arista's arrival, a detachment of sixty-three U.S. dragoons under Capt. Seth B. Thornton was sent to watch Mexican movements upriver. They engaged a larger party of Mexican regular troops near the settlement of Las Rucias. One officer, Lt. George T. Mason, was killed, as were two sergeants and eight privates, and the entire command was captured. Although Thornton reported that Arista personally had ensured that the prisoners were treated courteously, Taylor considered the fight to be an act of war by Mexico, and called on Governor Henderson to send four regiments of troops—two mounted and two infantry—to augment Walker. In a report to Adj. Gen. Roger Jones, Taylor wrote, "Hostilities may now be considered as commenced."[31]

The Mexicans agreed. On April 23 President Paredes issued a proclamation of defensive war. While he carefully phrased it to avoid a formal declaration, placing the burden of that act on the United States Congress, he nevertheless left no room for misunderstanding. He said that because of the acts of the United States up to this point, including the occupation of Padre Island, Point Isabel, and the right bank of the Rio Bravo del Norte (i.e. Rio

Grande) opposite Matamoros, the blockade of the Rio Grande, and the seizure of Laredo by U.S. forces, the United States had committed acts of war. "From this day commences a defensive war," he said, "and those points of our territory which are invaded or attacked will be energetically defended."[32]

Despite its bellicose tone, some of the wording indicates that Paredes, now that he was at the brink, had reassessed his position, because the proclamation gave him an opening for peace: if Taylor would simply pull back beyond the Nueces "the ancient limits of Texas," bloodshed might yet be avoided. In other words, Mexico was prepared to swallow its pride and recognize the loss of Texas as a *fait accompli*, provided the boundary was the Nueces.[33]

It was too late. Both sides had set their armies in motion, and neither could pull back with any semblance of honor. And in the nineteenth century, no government, least of all those of insecure new countries like the United States or Mexico, could hope to maintain public confidence if national honor was sacrificed.

3.
THE OPENING GUNS

ON PAPER, THE MEXICAN ARMY was formidable, yet its effectiveness was hampered by the generally chaotic conditions that prevailed in Mexico. Not only was the service divided by the various political rivalries among the generals, the vast size of Mexico and its lack of infrastructure fragmented the army to the point that drill, discipline, and a sense of mission were difficult, if not impossible, to maintain. The military academy at Chapultepec Castle, outside Mexico City, provided a thorough education, but had no program of recruitment or retention. Most young Mexican men were not interested in the military profession, and those that were found it easier to gain a commission by supporting a particular general in a political crisis than sitting through the three-year curriculum. Consequently, Chapultepec never instilled the level of training or purpose of its U.S. counterpart.[1]

Militarily, the United States was not prepared, because it suffered from a popular suspicion of standing professional armies and a misplaced confidence in the citizen-soldier concept. The army's authorized strength, 8,613 officers and men, was small enough, but at the beginning of 1846 it had more than three thousand vacancies. A generation had passed since the War of 1812, and veterans of that war were now late middle age or older. Such fighting as the U.S. Army had seen since then had been more in the nature of police actions against Indians. It was increasingly obvious that the war would be taken into Mexico, and the country had never mounted a major campaign beyond its own boundaries or immediate capabilities of support. Additionally, the American system of war management—if indeed a system really existed—depended more on political loyalties than on competence.[2]

But where Mexico's numerical strength was negated by the overall weakness of the system, the outward weakness of the United States was offset by several key factors. Despite political influences in war management, the regular officers of the U.S. Army, especially the younger ones, were well-trained specialists. Many were products of the yet untested United States Military Academy at West Point, where political influence allowed a potential student to gain entry, but, once admitted, the cadet kept his position entirely by his own merit. Although graduates of the antebellum academy lacked a sense of professionalism and discipline as understood by the twentieth-century army, nevertheless, having passed through the rigorous scientific approach to war laid down two decades earlier by Superintendent Sylvanus Thayer, they emerged skilled and capable. In reality, and despite occasional personality and ego clashes, the army General Taylor commanded in those first months was a highly efficient organization, considering its time and place.[3]

The industrial capacity of the United States, and recent advances in transportation and communications, added to its ability not only to assemble an army, but also to supply and equip it for an extended campaign over long distances. One key factor was weaponry. The Mexican infantry was armed with British East India surplus flintlocks, often double-charged, which were inaccurate as well as painful to fire. Cavalry generally carried lances, outdated carbines, and sabers. Much of the artillery dated from the Napoleonic era, calibers were not standardized, and the gun carriages were prone to breakdown. Most U.S. soldiers likewise used flintlock muskets, but were better trained and more skilled in their use. But while the flintlock was the standard issue, many troops were provided modern percussion-fired rifles and rifled muskets. The United States also had made great advances in gunnery, developing light, mobile "flying artillery," which could be easily and rapidly moved and aimed accurately over long ranges.

It would be safe to say that U.S. artillery was comparable, if not superior, to any in the world.[4]

The Napoleonic adage that an army "travels on its stomach" became evident during the Mexican War. Although there were occasional shortages, the United States Quartermaster and Commissary Departments managed to successfully establish huge depots on the Texas Gulf Coast, using steamships to supply the men with food and equipment. Enterprising businessmen and women followed the army deep into Mexico, offering the amenities the military did not provide. Mexico, on the other hand, was never able to develop an organized system. Supplies were requisitioned from the local population and paid for with government scrip of dubious value; consequently, the local population refused to sell. It was not uncommon to find Mexican soldiers poorly clad and hungry.[5]

Despite these obstacles, the Mexicans were hard at work preparing Matamoros for defense. The upper ferry across the Rio Grande was protected by Fort Paredes, an earthen construction comparable to Taylor's field work, capable of holding eight hundred men. Aside from the Casa Mata, an existing masonry blockhouse opposite Taylor's camp, the Mexicans erected two redoubts with crossing fire overlooking the lower ferry. Any gaps in the lines were plugged with gabions (wickerwork filled with dirt) and sand bags.

The Mexicans also had learned something about the situation in the U.S. camp, where squabbling had broken out among some of the ranking officers. A smoldering feud had existed since the previous fall between General Worth on the one hand, and General Taylor and Col. David E. Twiggs on the other. Worth held his rank by brevet, with the active rank of colonel. During one review Taylor had designated Twiggs, as senior colonel, to command the troops, which Worth protested, arguing that his brevet rank should have superseded that of Twiggs. In early April Worth learned that Taylor's decision had been upheld by President Polk. In a huff, he offered his resignation, which was promptly accepted, and Worth returned home.

Worth's departure delighted the Mexicans, who had been impressed by his soldierly bearing. Taylor, with his blunt, common-soldier style, struck them as a nonentity. They knew that another competent officer, Lt. Col. Ethan Allen Hitchcock, had been granted leave on the grounds of ill health, and that many of the higher-ranking officers in the camp were absent for various reasons. They were also aware that a large percentage of the soldiers were foreign born and, in the Mexican mind, could be classed as mercenaries or adventurers without real incentive to fight. Thus, they believed that they only needed to concern themselves with Taylor and could easily handle the situation. In this, they completely misjudged both General Taylor and his troops.[6]

The size and concentration of the Mexican army, which outnumbered Taylor's total strength by about three to two, worried some U.S. officers, who realized their own forces were spread dangerously thin. A large contingent of Mexicans already had crossed the river upstream from Taylor's camp, and there was a strong probability that the main force would cross downstream and sever communications with Point Isabel. At Point Isabel, Monroe had adequate supplies but would be unable to defend the depot against such a large force, whereas on the Rio Grande, Taylor had a formidable defense but only marginal supplies.[7]

The plain between Point Isabel and Matamoros was guarded by Walker's Rangers, sent by Major Monroe to watch for enemy movements and maintain communications with Taylor. On April 28 Walker took his most experienced men on a scout, leaving the camp defended by green recruits when it was attacked by *rancheros*. The Texans lost ten of the fifteen Rangers involved in the fight, including at least one who was lariated to death. The attack on Walker, together with reports of a large force of Mexican regulars crossing the river below Matamoros, convinced Monroe that the depot was threatened. He began strengthening the defenses and augmented his forces by pressing into service the officers and crews of ships in port. Late on the night of April 29, Walker and six Rangers slipped out of Point Isabel to advise General Taylor of the situation. About eight miles from the Rio Grande, they were confronted by a line of Mexican troops stretched across the prairie. After a quick conference, the Rangers charged. Before the surprised Mexicans could recover, they had broken the line and escaped. Soon they were within the safety of Taylor's camp.[8]

The line of troops that Walker had encountered was an advance contingent of the main Mexican army, which began crossing the river on April 30 at a ranch called Longoreño, about fifteen miles downstream from Taylor's camp at Fort Texas. Because only three barges were available, movement was slow, and Arista was not able to get his entire command across until the following day. Taylor knew that the Mexican army was experiencing shortages because of the U.S. blockade of the Rio Grande and correctly surmised that Arista hoped to disrupt communications, capture Point Isabel, and resupply from the depot there. Nevertheless, Taylor decided to delay any movement and concentrate on strengthening his fortifications until he was certain that Longoreño was the only crossing the Mexicans would make. Finally, on May 1, as Arista was getting the last of his troops across the river, Taylor decided to take the bulk of his forces back toward the coast. He intended to protect the depot and bring back supplies to Fort Texas. The fort, now capable of withstanding a short siege, was left under command of Maj. Jacob Brown, Seventh Infantry, with about five hundred men. Its artillery defense consisted of four 18-pounders and a field battery. The remaining two thousand men left about 3:30 P.M., marching some eighteen miles before going into camp. They arrived in Point Isabel about noon the following day, much to the frustration of Arista, who had been unable to intercept them because of the delays in crossing the river.

Initially, Taylor intended to remain in Point Isabel until ordnance supplies—and hopefully more troops—arrived from New Orleans.[9] On May 3, however, the U.S. troops camped by the bay heard cannon fire from the direction of the Rio Grande. Captain Henry wrote, "The heavy, booming sound of cannon came rolling in from the direction of the fort, opposite Matamoras [*sic*]. The camp was wild with excitement; we knew our gallant fellows were resisting a bombardment, and all were anxious to fly to their rescue."[10]

Almost all. "What General Taylor's feelings were during this suspense I do not know," Grant commented years later, "but for myself, a young second-lieutenant who had never heard a hostile gun before, I felt sorry that I had enlisted."[11]

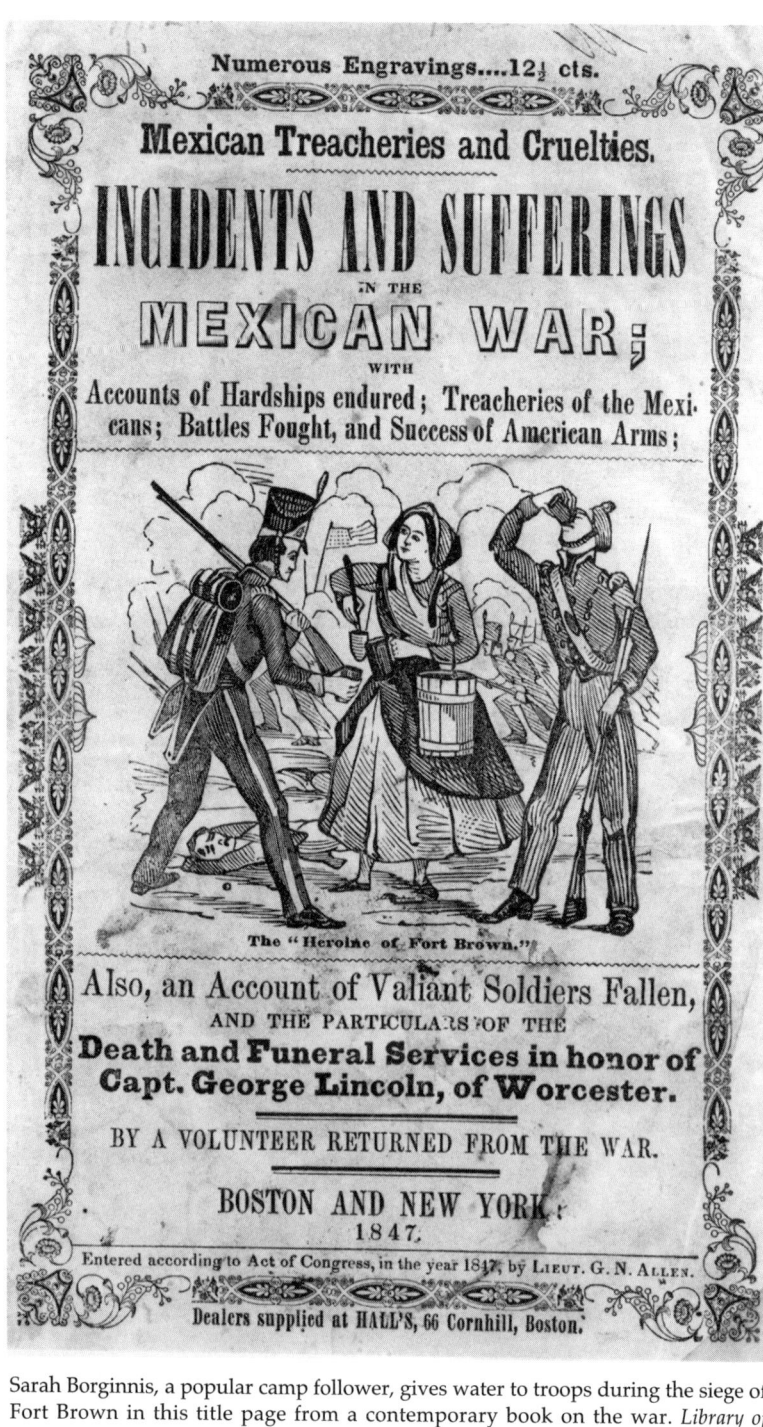

Sarah Borginnis, a popular camp follower, gives water to troops during the siege of Fort Brown in this title page from a contemporary book on the war. *Library of Congress.*

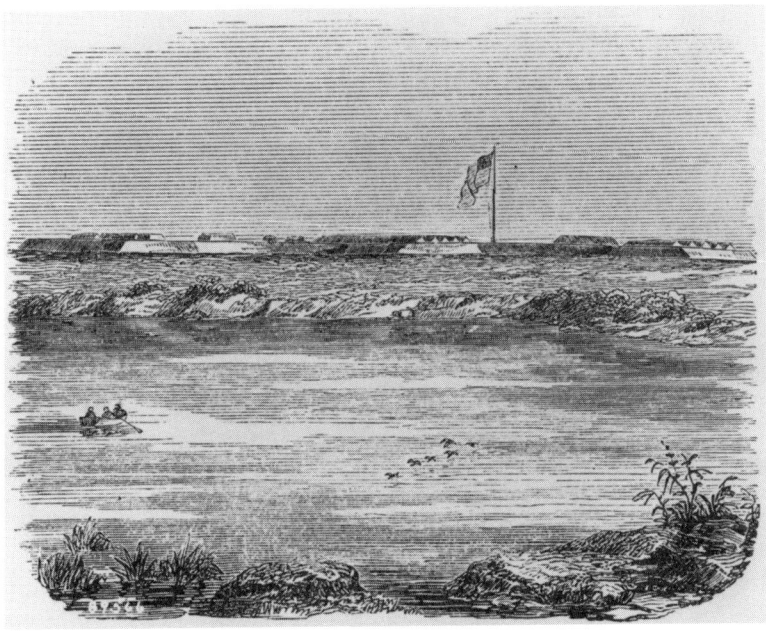

The earthworks at Fort Brown are shown in a contemporary engraving published in several accounts of the war in 1847 and 1848. One course of the wall and a bastion point are still preserved on the Brownsville Municipal Golf Course. *W. S. Henry,* Campaign Sketches of the War with Mexico *(New York: Harper & Brothers, Publishers, 1847), opposite p. 103.*

The bombardment had begun at 5 A.M. that day when the Mexicans opened fire from a sandbag battery of seven guns. Brown, a fifty-eight-year-old veteran, who had joined the army as a private during the War of 1812, immediately ordered his own batteries manned and returned fire for half an hour until the Mexican battery fell silent. The Mexicans then removed the guns from the exposed sand bag battery and commenced firing from the lower fort and a mortar battery. Although the shelling generally was accurate, it did little harm to the U.S. earthworks. Brown then ordered one battery to fire into the town, taking care to respect the flags of the various consulates. Believing that the bombardment was the prelude to an assault, he kept his men busy throughout the day, strengthening the curtain wall and gate, which were finally completed that night.

THEN AND NOW

Except for brief periods, Fort Brown remained an active military post from its founding in 1846 until its ultimate abandonment in 1944. Taylor's earthworks were vacated in favor of an open cantonment soon after the Mexican War. The antebellum structures were destroyed during the Civil War, and the post was extensively reconstructed beginning in 1007. In 1948 the War Assets Administration deeded the post to the Brownsville School District, which, together with the City of Brownsville and the federal government, demolished most of the military structures (both historic and twentieth century) to make way for a junior college, various municipal buildings, and the customs and immigration station for Gateway International Bridge. Today, Fort Brown is the seat of Texas Southmost College/ University of Texas at Brownsville, and only a few of the military structures remain. A small portion of Taylor's original earthworks survive behind the fort, in the southwest corner of the Brownsville Municipal Golf Course just beyond the driving range. An upended Mexican War–era cannon is embedded in concrete. Little is being done to preserve the site from deterioration. A historical marker is located at the Fort Brown Civic Center on International Boulevard, the site of the 1867 parade ground.

The site of Thornton's Skirmish is on U.S. 281 twenty-one miles west of Brownsville. It is designated by a roadside park with shelter, a cannon with a founder's date of 1853 mounted in concrete, and a state historical marker.

The Mexicans ceased firing around 7:30 P.M. The fourteen-hour bombardment had claimed only one casualty, a sergeant named Weigart, who found no peace even in death. Killed instantly by an exploding shell, his body was laid out on the surgeon's table, where it was torn apart by another shell. When he was buried, a third shell exploded on the grave, exhuming the remains. Several U.S. soldiers were wounded and were nursed by an attractive, muscular, six-foot-tall camp follower named Sarah Borginnis, popularly called the Great Western after the most famous steamship of the period.[12] Mexican losses for the day amounted to one sergeant and two artillerymen.

Brown ordered one battery to fire into the city with hot shot— solid shot that had been heated in an oven—in an effort to distract the Mexicans by burning some of their buildings. Without a conventional hot shot oven, however, he could not obtain the desired temperature. The Mexicans then concentrated their fire on that battery. At 10 P.M. Brown suspended his fire in order to conserve ammunition. Mexican fire tapered off and ceased entirely around midnight.[13]

General Taylor, meanwhile, sent Walker and a detail of Rangers, with cavalry escort, to try and open communications with Brown. The cavalry returned after reconnoitering the Mexican positions, while the Rangers reached the fort a little after 2 A.M. on May 4. After making one unsuccessful attempt to get back to Point Isabel, Walker finally departed and reached Taylor later in the morning. Satisfied that Fort Texas was in no immediate danger, he decided to await expected reinforcements from New Orleans, then relieve Brown.[14]

In the fort, Brown kept the men busy repairing and strengthening the defenses, under the immediate supervision of Capt. J. K. F. Mansfield, the army's engineer, whom Taylor had left behind for that purpose. Elsewhere, though, General Arista was annoyed by the continual U.S. presence opposite Matamoros. Early on May 5, he sent Ampudia with a large contingent of troops, including sappers and artillery, to attack the fort. Mexican fire resumed at 5 A.M. and daylight revealed a new battery behind the fort, with a portion of Ampudia's troops concentrated around it. Although this could catch the fort in a cross-fire, fire from the Mexican batteries was only sporadic. After noon, however, the bombardment stepped up, then ceased altogether. Brown believed the Mexicans were preparing for an assault. This seemed to be confirmed when the Mexicans began moving around the outside of the works, as though trying to select the best point of attack. Lt. Charles Hanson, Seventh Infantry, received permission to lead a party of dragoons on reconnaissance. The Mexicans spotted them, but despite efforts to cut them off, Hanson managed to lead his men safely back to the fort. Although the Mexicans now completely encircled the fort, the assault did not materialize. Even so, Brown ordered a gun fired at regular intervals, a prearranged signal to Taylor that he now was under a regular siege.

The Mexicans began a heavy bombardment on May 6, all batteries hammering away at the fort with hot shot and shell. Mortar

A shell explosion mortally wounds Maj. Jacob Brown during the bombardment of Fort Texas. After the defeat of Arista's army and the capture of Matamoros, Taylor renamed the post Fort Brown. *John Frost,* Pictorial History of Mexico and the Mexican War *(Philadelphia: Charles Desilver, 1862), Author's Collection.*

fire rained in, tearing tents to pieces, and killing and wounding the artillery horses. Brown held fire, conserving his ammunition for the anticipated assault. At 10 A.M., while he was supervising work on the defenses, he was struck by a cannonball that tore off part of his right leg. He was carried to a bomb-proof shelter, where a surgeon completed the amputation. Command of the fort fell to Capt. Edgar S. Hawkins.[15]

Soon after Brown fell, large parties of Mexican infantry and cavalry began moving on the fort from the rear. A battery commanded by Lt. Braxton Bragg opened fire with canister and the assault parties withdrew. The bombardment continued until about 12:30 P.M., then began tapering off. A little after 4 P.M. the Mexicans called for a parley, and two officers approached with a white flag. They carried a note from Arista calling on the U.S. troops to surrender in order to avoid further bloodshed. Although unable to get an exact translation, Hawkins understood the meaning and sent Arista a polite refusal. The Mexicans then resumed firing with the most intense bombardment yet.[16]

4.
PALO ALTO AND RESACA DE LA PALMA

BROWN'S SIGNAL GUNS CREATED a new sense of urgency in Point Isabel. At 3 P.M. on May 3 Taylor issued orders to march for Fort Texas. He told the troops that they might have to drive the Mexicans from the route of march, but that he had every confidence in their abilities and knew the outcome of any battle would be victory.[1] The orders encouraged the troops. According to Henry, "The order, in advance, announced a victory. There was no doubt expressed by it. Commanding a much inferior force, composed of troops few of whom had ever 'smelt gunpowder,' our brave general, nevertheless, speaks to them as old veterans."[2]

Arista, meanwhile, was unfamiliar with the terrain and tried to find the best spot to cut the road Taylor would use between Point Isabel and Matamoros. The Mexican army camped on high ground overlooking the plain of Palo Alto the night of May 7. The following morning, scouts brought word that the Americans were coming. Arista broke camp, made final preparations, threw a line across the road, and waited. Despite an outward bravado borne of numerical superiority, morale in the army was low. Three changes in command inside of a month had undermined the average soldier's faith in his leaders. General Ampudia, resentful of his subordinate status, undermined Arista at every turn. Arista himself was under pressure from the government to take early, decisive action and was not certain that he was ready.[3] As one contemporary

The two faces of Maj. Gen. Mariano Arista, commander of the Mexican Army of the North. A fanciful contemporary American sketch, right, depicts him as heavily mustachioed and piratical, a stereotype of Mexicans based largely on the infamous "Black Legend" of the Elizabethan past. An accurate portrait, left, shows the fair-skinned, red-headed Arista to be well-groomed and clean-shaven, as were most Mexican officers of the era. *Right, N. C. Brooks,* Complete History of the Mexican War *(Philadelphia: Grigg, Elliott, 1849), Author's Collection. Left, Nettie Lee Benson Collection, University of Texas at Austin.*

Mexican writer noted, "The spirit of discord raising its head, grew rapidly, and these shameful dissensions were, as we will see, one of the principal causes of the disasters which precipitated the long series of our defeats."[4]

Late that morning, Walker located the Mexican campsite and found they had moved. Many thought they had withdrawn to avoid a fight. After marching about twelve miles, however, the advance guard reported Arista's troops gathered in force. "Debouching from a point of mesquite, the masses of the enemy were apparent, less than a mile distance, and occupying a front of nearly a mile and a half," Henry wrote.[5] Pvt. Barna Upton, Third Infantry, added, "We advanced about half a mile, halted by a pond, and after getting water to drink and resting a little, our little

Army forced its line of battle and advanced to meet the enemy. They were six thousand strong, while we numbered but little more than two thousand."[6]

Arista had chosen his position well. The field at Palo Alto was essentially flat and featureless except for stands of mesquite. However, barely visible low spots drew water from higher ground, which, after a rain, became virtually impassable bogs. It had rained the week before, and Arista used the soggy ground to his advantage. He placed himself in a defensive position, his line extending from a bog to a mesquite thicket, thereby throwing the burden of attack to Taylor. Part of his cavalry covered his right, while an entire cavalry brigade under General Torrejón protected the left, separated from the infantry regiments by yet another artillery battery.[7]

His dispositions completed, Arista rode along the line, addressing each unit about the glory and gratitude they would receive after the coming victory. "His remarks," according to a contemporary Mexican account, "were received with enthusiasm, the banners floated to the wind, the soldiers stood to their arms, the horses pawed the ground, the bands performed inspiring and beautiful music, and shouts filled the air of 'Viva la Republica,' as if bearing up to the throne of a just God, the cry of vengeance raised by an offended nation."[8]

On the U.S. side, Taylor was in no hurry. He sat sidesaddle on his horse, "Old Whitey," chewed a piece of tobacco, and pondered the situation. He allowed the men to fill their canteens at one of the ponds, which gave him more time to complete his deployment. His most vulnerable spot was his three-hundred-wagon supply train, and he realized that the Mexican cavalry might flank him and take the train. He detached a squadron of dragoons and two pieces of artillery to protect the train, although he knew this would cost him valuable troops. Their canteens full, the U.S. soldiers resumed a slow march. When they had gone about three quarters of a mile, the Mexican artillery opened fire.[9]

The cannonade was Private Upton's first taste of war. He remarked that they shoot dreadful careless in battle. The balls were constantly hissing over our heads or mowing their way through the tall grass, and it was astonishing how few struck our ranks. I noticed one ball spinning its way through the grass close to the ground with the swiftness of the swiftest [railroad] car. It passed about six feet from me. The men who were in the path dodged it in safety.[10]

The Americans advanced a bit farther; then their artillery returned fire. The batteries were commanded by Bvt. Maj. Samuel Ringgold, Third Artillery, who had helped develop the "flying artillery" concept. As the U.S. shots mowed through his ranks, Arista knew he would have to attack. His infantry, however, was unable to maneuver in the chaparral, so he ordered Torrejón's cavalry to advance. Taylor's Eighth Infantry Regiment formed a hollow square to take the assault while Ringgold's batteries slammed shells into the oncoming lancers. Arista had made a dreadful mistake. He had placed Torrejón in a position where he had to attack through an opening between a mesquite thicket and a bog. His cavalry was funneling through this opening when it caught the full force of the U.S. gunnery.

The U.S. infantry then pivoted to support Ringgold, which gave the foot soldiers a clear field of fire to open up at the Mexican cavalry with their muskets. With no room to maneuver, Torrejón fell back. To the Mexicans, the infantry move appeared to be an effort to flank Arista's left. They turned to meet it, which did nothing except further hinder their artillery. Meanwhile, Capt. James Duncan had caught the Mexican turn, moved his guns into position, and opened fire. In one last effort, Arista sent his cavalry to take the American supply train; the dispirited horsemen fell back after initial contact with the train's guards.

Muzzle flashes from the artillery set the prairie grass on fire. Some U.S. soldiers were severely burned, but with the wind at the Americans' backs, the fire swept toward the Mexican lines. Many of the Mexican wounded died in the flames. Smoke blinded men on both sides and obstructed Taylor's view of the Mexican position. At this point a charge would have overwhelmed the Mexicans, but Taylor feared that committing the necessary number of troops would leave his train inadequately protected. He

Maj. Samuel Ringgold, who helped develop the winning concept of flying artillery, was a popular officer, whose death from wounds received at Palo Alto was mourned by the troops. *Library of Congress.*

tried to take Arista's train when the smoke cleared, but found it heavily defended.[11]

It was growing late, and the U.S. advance began to slow. The Mexicans were tired of being hammered by long-range U.S. artillery. Their own guns did not reach far enough to silence the enemy, and they would be cut to pieces if they charged. "Their officers made an attempt to charge upon us but the havoc would have been so great that their soldiers could not be made to advance," Grant wrote. "Some of the prisoners . . . say that their officers cut and slashed among them with their Sabres at a dreadful rate to make them advance but it was no use, they could not come."[12]

Realizing any further effort was futile, Arista broke off the action and withdrew some distance down the road. Details were able to recover some of the wounded but had to leave those who died on the field or in the hospitals. Mexican losses were estimated at about five hundred. Four United States soldiers died outright, and forty-three officers and men were wounded, some mortally. Two were listed as missing. Ringgold had been mortally wounded when a Mexican cannonball ripped through his horse from one side to the other, taking his thighs with it. Ringgold was popular, and the soldiers mourned his loss. Capt. John Page of the infantry died after another cannonball tore away his lower jaw and shattered the roof of his mouth. Because most of the battle had been fought with artillery, the wounds generally were severe, and the surgeons worked all night amputating shattered limbs.[13]

Tactically, the battle of Palo Alto was a draw. Both armies remained intact, and the Mexicans had done little more than withdraw and go into camp beyond range of the U.S. guns. Taylor, however, held the field, and his troops' morale was high. That was not the case with the Mexicans. The ordinary soldiers felt betrayed. Expecting an overwhelming victory, the withdrawal from Palo Alto appeared a defeat, and this could have only come because their officers had failed them. They already dreaded the next encounter with the U.S. troops.[14] "After this moment they cried as one voice *that they had been sold out*, and branded His Excellency the general-in-chief as a traitor," wrote an anonymous Mexican officer. "The admonitions and strong representations of the officers stopped the murmurings; but the disgust existed, the lack of confidence continued, and with these elements the division prepared to meet the ninth [of May]."[15]

The next morning, scouts reported that the Mexican army was withdrawing down the road toward Matamoros. Taylor held an officers' call, where the majority, citing the numbers that still favored Arista, urged him to remain in place until the expected reinforcements arrived. The younger officers, however, urged him to chase the Mexicans and finish them. After listening to everyone's opinion, Taylor told his officers, "Gentlemen, you will prepare your commands to move forward."[16] As the U.S. forces got ready to follow the Mexicans, Captain Henry rode back over the battlefield and saw the grim results of the American artillery. "There were heaps of dead lying hither and yon, with the most ghastly wounds I ever saw," he wrote. American soldiers gave food and water to one wounded Mexican they found on the field. Elsewhere, a dog stood by the body of his master and could not be induced to leave.[17]

TEXAS AND THE MEXICAN WAR

THEN AND NOW

Palo Alto Battlefield National Historic Site is between Brownsville and Los Fresnos and can be reached by taking FM 511 from U.S. Expressway 77/83 or FM 1847 from Los Fresnos. The National Park Service is presently developing the site with a visitors' center and interpretive trails. The battlefield is the best-preserved Mexican War site in the United States and the only Mexican War site in the National Park System. It also is one of the few battlefields in the system that is in essentially the same condition as the day the battle was fought. The National Park Service's preservation efforts are directed not only to its historic significance, but also to the abundant native plant and animal life.

FM 1847 retraces the old road both Taylor and Arista used. Resaca de la Palma is reached by driving due south on 1847, which becomes Paredes Line Road upon entering Brownsville. The battlefield is unrecognizable because it is covered with extensive residential and commercial development. The only undeveloped section is an old polo field to the left of the bridge where the road crosses the resaca. This, however, is where some of the heaviest fighting occurred. On the left, about a mile north of the resaca crossing where so much blood was shed, a Mexican War-era cannon has been placed in a concrete mount. The historical marker has been removed.

The site of Camp Belknap, where as many as seven thousand soldiers lived in deplorable conditions, is on the south side of State Highway 4 about eighteen miles east of Brownsville and is designated by a historical marker. Five miles further east, where the highway enters Boca Chica, a granite centennial state historical marker points out two rows of pilings running parallel to the road on the north side. Those closest to the road are said to date from the Civil War, while the second row, about a thousand feet beyond, is purportedly the remains of a pontoon bridge built during the Mexican War to transport troops and equipment over the marshy ground. The information on the marker should be taken with caution because its accuracy is questionable.

Arista had begun his withdrawal at 6 A.M., sending cavalry to cover his retreat, and recalling the troops who were still besieging Fort Texas. The clumps of mesquite thicket scattered here and there along the plain at Palo Alto turned into dense chaparral about half a mile down the road. After a four-hour march, Arista decided to make a stand where the road crossed Resaca de la Palma, an ancient channel of the Rio Grande. Cutting through the chaparral and obliquely across the road, it was a shallow ravine, dry except for some rain-filled ponds. The banks were lined with mesquite thickets that would limit the effectiveness of the U.S. artillery. On this terrain, the Mexican soldier could fight as he fought best—in close combat, face-to-face with the enemy. Sappers and infantry were placed along the right, using the bank as a breastwork, with coastal defense infantry (*Guardia Costa*) to the left. Infantry and irregular troops under Gen. Antonio Canales hovered in the chaparral to the rear, while the cavalry and train were in a clearing some three hundred yards to the rear. Sharpshooters were placed in the mesquite thickets with a clear view of the road. To force the Americans into the line of infantry, Arista positioned his artillery across the road.[18]

The U.S. advance was slow and deliberate, the scouts keeping just behind the Mexican rear guard. Taylor halted his men for two or three hours to wait for the scouts to report back. They said that the chaparral was clear for about five miles. At 1 P.M. the army resumed the march and had covered the distance when the advance guard reported the Mexicans in front. Capt. William W. Mackall drew a quick map so that Taylor would have some idea of the terrain, and some of the advance guard moved forward to draw fire and determine the position of the guns. Now that he had the information he needed, Taylor deployed infantry to flank the Mexican left and right and the dragoons to charge the guns at the center. First, however, he sent Capt. Randolph Ridgely, who now commanded Ringgold's battery, to see if he could blow a hole in the Mexican artillery position. Ridgely had placed his guns and was preparing to fire when a column of lancers emerged from the chaparral and came down on him. In desperation, Ridgely wheeled his guns and fired point-blank into the oncoming horsemen. The lancers fell back.[19]

Taylor ordered Capt. Charles May to take a company of dragoons and overrun the Mexican batteries. As May rode up to the line, Ridgely shouted, "Hold on, Charley, till I draw their fire!"[20] Then he let loose a round, which the Mexicans answered. Taking advantage of the reload time, May's men charged. As the lead horses reached the ravine, Lt. Zebulon M. P. Inge turned to wave

The dashing, impetuous Capt. Charles May became a hero when popular imagination credited him with overrunning a Mexican battery and capturing Maj. Gen. Romulo Diaz de la Vega. In fact, May's unsupported charge nearly ended in disaster and the guns and general were captured by others. *N. C. Brooks,* Complete History of the Mexican War *(Philadelphia: Grigg, Elliott, 1849), Author's Collection.*

the others on. By then, however, the Mexican gunners had reloaded and let loose a barrage of grape and canister. The blast of metal tore through the U.S. ranks, knocking eighteen horses and seven men into a bloody heap. Among the dead was Lieutenant Inge. May led the remainder through a line of batteries, momentarily startling the gunners, and found himself face-to-face with General Díaz de la Vega. Mexican infantry surrounded the U.S. dragoons, and the gunners had recovered their composure and were returning to their pieces. May wheeled his horse around, broke back through the Mexican line, and retreated.[21]

Watching the whole affair, Taylor was furious that May had allowed himself to be trapped. Turning to Col. William Belknap he shouted, "Take those guns, and by God, keep them!" Belknap's Eighth Infantry charged down the road.[22]

"Grape shot and musket balls were let fly from both sides making dreadful havoc," Grant wrote. "Our men continued to advance . . . in spite of their shots, to the very mouths of the cannons and killed and took prisoner the Mexicans with them." They also captured General Díaz de la Vega, although May later got the credit. The Americans captured nine Mexican guns, turned them around, and opened fire. Grant found a clear space and charged through with his company, capturing a wounded Mexican colonel and several soldiers. He was congratulating himself when an American private came from ahead with a badly wounded U.S. officer—the ground had been taken already. "This left no doubt in my mind that the battle of Resaca de la Palma would have been won, just as it was, if I had not been there," he remarked.[23]

The Mexican infantry was spread out into such a long line that many soldiers were not even involved in the fight. They could only stand on the flanks and watch the center as the U.S. troops tore the heart out of the army. In one last effort to save the battle, Arista personally took command of the lancers and led a final, hopeless charge. The U.S. firepower made quick work of the effort, and he was forced to retreat. Although the troops admired their general's courage, they had had enough. The U.S. infantry made a general charge with bayonets, and the Mexican line collapsed. Panic-stricken soldiers fled the remaining three miles to the river, where an estimated three hundred men drowned in a desperate attempt to cross back to Matamoros. The Army of the North had been destroyed.[24]

Inside Fort Texas, the men could only guess at the outcome of the guns they had heard over the last two days. On the night of May 8, a Mexican deserter had appeared and told them about the fight at Palo Alto, but had few details. The next day, the siege parties were gone, and the bombardment from Matamoros received little notice, as the garrison listened to the guns at Resaca de la Palma. The only noteworthy incident was when Major Brown died in the bomb-proof shelter. Late that afternoon, hordes of fleeing Mexican soldiers broke through the chaparral around the fort making for the river, and the guns in Matamoros fell silent. The cheering U.S. soldiers turned the fort's guns on the fugitives, but their fire had little effect.[25]

Now that there appeared to be a break in the fighting, Taylor settled down to the administrative duties of a commanding general. He traveled back to Point Isabel to confer with Commodore Conner on the reduction of the river towns of Burita, Matamoros, and Camargo. While there, he designated the defense work at the depot as Fort Polk, as "a mark of respect to the Chief Magistrate of the republic."[26] Back on the Rio Grande, he changed the name of the fieldwork from Fort Texas to Fort Brown, in honor of its defender. He also arranged for Thornton and his men to be paroled in exchange for Mexican prisoners. The parole allowed the prisoners of each side to return to their own lines as non-combatants until formal exchange had been made. While some of the Mexicans accepted it, General Díaz de la Vega and others refused. They knew their own people well enough to know that the parole would not be honored in Mexico, and they would be immediately pressed back into service regardless of any agreements. Taylor sent them to New Orleans for internment with a note indicating he expected the Mexican prisoners to be treated with the same exemplary courtesy they had extended to his men in captivity. The hapless Captain Clay, whose crippled schooner *Susannah* had been seized months earlier, was released from confinement in San Fernando on General Taylor's orders.[27]

Recruits drill on the beach as volunteers arrive to augment Taylor's army. The United States relied heavily on ill-trained and poorly disciplined citizen volunteers for the bulk of its fighting power. *John Frost,* Pictorial History of Mexico and the Mexican War *(Philadelphia: Charles Desilver, 1862), Author's Collection.*

5.
OCCUPATION

EVEN AS THE TWO ARMIES were fighting at Resaca de la Palma, President Polk met with his cabinet. Unaware of events on the Rio Grande, the main concern was breaking what appeared to be an impasse between the United States and Mexico. "I said that in my opinion we had ample cause of war," Polk wrote in his diary, "and that it was impossible that we could stand in *statu quo*, or that I could remain silent much longer; that I thought it was my duty to send a message to Congress very soon and recommend definite measures." All agreed that if the Mexicans committed any hostile act, the president would ask Congress for a declaration of war. At 6 P.M. the same day, however, Adjutant General Jones arrived with dispatches from Taylor describing the attack on Thornton's men several weeks earlier. Polk now had his justification, and immediately summoned the cabinet, which unanimously agreed that a war message should be sent to Congress. When the meeting broke up at 10 P.M., the president set to work on his message. It was submitted to Congress at noon on Monday, May 11. The same afternoon, the House of Representatives approved a declaration of war by a vote of 173 to 14, with 20 abstentions. On Tuesday, the Senate approved the declaration by a vote of 42 to 2.[1]

Five days later, the cabinet assembled to discuss the prosecution of the war. Polk proposed to move against Santa Fe and Chihuahua, conquering Mexico's northernmost provinces, and occupying the Mexican interior adjacent to the lower Rio Grande (or, as Polk called it, "the lower Del Norte"). He had already decided to call on the southern and western states for twenty thousand volunteers, and now he decided to call an additional thirty thousand from the remaining states and territories, "so as to make each feel an interest in the war."[2]

On May 23 the mail brought reports of Taylor's victories at Palo Alto and Resaca de la Palma, which were confirmed by Taylor's official dispatches two days later. Polk found these victories useful in two ways: they justified the war, and they helped him decide what to do with Maj. Gen. Winfield Scott, the difficult but popular general-in-chief of the army. The two men detested each other. The arrogant, egotistical Scott saw himself as a contender for the presidency. His attitude toward his commander-in-chief, alternately demanding and condescending, infuriated Polk, who initially had planned to place him in command of the troops on the Rio Grande, as much to get him out of Washington and public view as for any other reason. Now, however, Taylor was the popular hero, and the public would not tolerate his removal from the theater of war. Nor could he serve under Scott's immediate command—assuming he had equal rank. Accordingly, the Machiavellian president nominated Taylor for the brevet rank of major general, and congress was quick to approve. Polk would keep Scott in the capital on a tight rein while Taylor had the glory—for the time being, at least.[3]

Taylor, meanwhile, had crossed the Rio Grande with Conner's assistance and had occupied Matamoros without resistance in the wake of the retreating Mexican army. Short of troops, he presumed on his authority to call on the governors of Texas and Louisiana for five thousand volunteers. Besides volunteers, federal troops began arriving, along with steamers capable of transporting troops and equipment up the river to Matamoros, and even as far as Camargo. Pursuing Polk's plan of separating the northern provinces, Taylor proposed to move against the fortified city of Monterrey. This meant he would have to first occupy Reynosa, some forty miles upriver from Matamoros, then move on to Camargo, where he would establish a large depot as a staging area for Monterrey. By June 3 he had some eight thousand men under his command, but many were six-month volunteers whose enlistments would expire before they even became acclimated to the region or accustomed to the military. Consequently, he decided to retain them in service beyond their enlistments, establishing them in decent camps and getting them properly trained.[84]

An assembly depot had been established at Brazos Santiago. As the new troops arrived, they either took steamers or marched to any of several camps upriver.[5] Brazos Santiago did nothing to build the enthusiasm of the troops for Texas or the coming campaign. Upon arriving there from West Point, Bvt. Second Lt. George B. McClellan, Corps of Engineers, called it

probably the very worst port that could be found on the whole American coast. We are encamped on an island which is nothing more than a sand bar, perfectly barren, utterly destitute of any sign of vegetation. . . . Whenever a strong breeze blows the sand flies along in perfect clouds, filling your tent, eyes and everything else. . . . The only good thing about this place is bathing in the surf. The water which we drink is obtained by digging a hole large enough to contain a barrel in which the water collects. You must dig until you find water, then "work-in" the barrel until it is well down. This water is very bad. It is brackish and unhealthy. The island is often overflowed [by the tide] to the depth of one or two feet.[6]

Barna Upton noted that dysentery was prevalent in Matamoros, a problem that one volunteer surgeon attributed to poorly prepared food. The common cures, a mixture of sulfates of copper and opium, and acetate of lead and opium, were probably more dangerous than the disease. The abundance of fresh fruit and vegetables that Mexican vendors brought into the American camps for sale caused contradictory problems. One the one hand, many U.S. soldiers, unused to such variety, gorged themselves to the point of illness. On the other, the Commissary Department (rudimentary and inept throughout much of the nineteenth century) failed to purchase and issue fruit and vegetables as part of the regular ration, and scurvy appeared among the troops in Matamoros.[7]

To soldiers from the northern United States, the summer heat and the lack of potable water were unendurable. "We marched about five miles [on the road from Matamoros to Reynosa] without any water except such as was occasionally to be found in a mud hole in the road which was very seldom," 2d Lt. Rankin Dilworth of the First Infantry recorded. "At twelve we halted for a rest on the side of a pond of hot water; and remained till two P.M. temperature 120 degrees. . . . Our men when in Iowa or Wisconsin Territories could march ten or twelve miles without [water], but here too [sic] or three miles is sufficient to exhaust them."[8]

Because the volunteer troops were organized by the states, their officers were chosen according to the laws of that particular state. In some cases, the governor appointed the officers, but more often they were elected. Consequently, they exercised very little authority over their unruly troops, who considered themselves free citizens not subject to the discipline of military service. Their objection to army routine even extended to camp sanitation, and as a result disease was rampant among their units. Likewise, the volunteers viewed themselves as entitled to spoils of war; plundering of the local citizens was chronic. Writing in Matamoros in July, Captain Henry remarked, "Of late there have been several disgraceful riots in the city, in which some of the volunteers were conspicuous, arising from the lax state of discipline in some of the regiments."[9]

The old problem of religion, which Taylor had worked so hard to quell among his troops and with the local population, aggravated the existing tensions. Although the regular army contained a sizeable number of Roman Catholics, the volunteers were almost exclusively Protestant militants, who viewed Roman Catholicism as heretical and idolatrous. Roman Catholic citizens and clergy were routinely abused and religious sites were desecrated, raising the possibility that Mexican propagandists might turn the war into a religious crusade. Apprised of the situation, President Polk secured the services of two Jesuits, who joined the army as auxiliary chaplains.[10] This action, innocuous enough, nonetheless infuriated some of the Protestants. "The idea of associating our government with any seat of the church especially one of the most despotic and monarchistic; I regard as encroaching on our Constitutional liberty," an Ohio Volunteer officer complained in his diary.[11]

Bvt. 2nd Lt. U. S. Grant regarded the Mexican War as unjust and came to believe that the Civil War was a sort of national punishment. *U.S. Military Academy Archives.*

The Texans were particularly troublesome, given their long-standing feuds with Mexico, and the fact that some had personal grievances stemming from their capture at Mier or Santa Fe and subsequent imprisonment earlier in the decade. In a letter to Julia Dent, Grant wrote:

Since we have been in Matamoras [*sic*] a great many murders have been committed, and what is strange there seems to be but very weak means made use of to prevent frequent repetitions. Some of the volunteers and about all the Texans seem to think it perfectly right to impose upon the people of a conquered City to any extent, and even to murder them where the act can be covered by the dark. And how much they seem to enjoy acts of violence too![12]

Texans also were perhaps the most unsoldierly in organization and appearance. They were accustomed to the easy familiarity of their traditional Rangers, where command and obedience were based on mutual respect. In July the various Ranger companies were consolidated as the First Texas Mounted Rifles and taken into federal service as part of the state's quota of volunteer troops. One of their most respected leaders, Jack Hays, was appointed colonel, and Sam Walker was named lieutenant colonel. One volunteer from Louisiana described the Texas camp in Matamoros as consisting of:

Texas Ranger Capt. Ben McCulloch took up the slack in scouting and reconnaissance following Samuel Walker's transfer to the Mounted Rifles. McCulloch's men not only sought out the Mexican forces, but also a Comanche raiding party party that depredated the Rio Grande region in the summer of 1846. This photograph was taken about a decade later, and shows McCulloch with the beard that became fashionable in the 1850s. During the Mexican War he was clean-shaven. *Texas State Library and Archives Commission.*

Men in groups with long beards and moustaches, dressed in every variety of garment, with one exception, the slouched hat, the unmistakable uniform of a Texas Ranger, and a belt of pistols around their waists, were occupied drying their blankets, cleaning and fixing their guns, and some employed cooking at different fires, while others were grooming their horses. A rougher looking set we never saw. They were without tents, and a miserable shed afforded them the only shelter.[13]

Not all Texans created mayhem. Hays, Walker, and most of their company commanders were from the area around San Antonio and South Central Texas. Mostly young and unattached, they were veterans of countless frontier battles, many of whom nursed grievances against Mexico. Among the most volatile was the company commanded by Capt. Ben McCulloch. By contrast, the men of Col. George T. Wood's Regiment of Texas Rangers were largely from East Texas and understood little of the quarrels with Mexico. Generally family men who left home and farm to volunteer for patriotic reasons, they kept to camp and minded their own business. On July 4, while McCulloch's men plundered and barbecued every head of civilian livestock they could find, the East Texans at Fort Brown attended a reading of the Declaration of Independence and listened to patriotic speeches.[14]

The idleness of the summer undermined morale. Many of the volunteers were ill with unknown fevers, and even the healthy ones began to consider their own mortality. "All is dull and gloomy," James K. Holland of Wood's Regiment wrote in his diary, "becoming tired of a stationary life—want to be moving—if there is no fighting to be done—as there seems to be—we are all willing to go home."[15]

While the United States went on a full war footing, Mexico slipped into a period of indecision that resulted in confused signals reaching Washington. On June 6, President Paredes asked for a full declaration of war against the United States. Congress, however, demurred, instead declaring a state of defensive war for the purpose of repelling an invader. Even then, the response was lukewarm, and Paredes was unable to generate either funds or enthusiasm. U.S. diplomats continued more or less in their usual functions and reported that Mexico might be receptive to peace. These events were followed with great interest, not only in Washington, but also in Havana, where the ousted Mexican president, Antonio López de Santa Anna, was spending his latest period of exile. As early as February, while Taylor was still in Corpus Christi, Polk had been advised that Santa Anna, if restored to power, favored a negotiated settlement with the United States. Now that Paredes and the monarchists were clearly losing favor, Polk believed the time had come to assist Santa Anna in a return to power. He sent a naval officer, Capt. Alexander Slidell Mackenzie, to Havana to discuss the possibility.[16]

Mackenzie and Santa Anna met on July 6 and 7. Mackenzie advised Santa Anna that the navy was ordered to allow him through the blockade, and would suspend all operations except the naval blockade, once Santa Anna returned to power and announced that Mexico would negotiate. U.S. terms, which Mackenzie was not supposed to reveal, but did anyway, included no indemnity against Mexico other than a settlement of existing U.S. claims, purchase of the disputed sub-Nueces territory of Texas, and purchase of New Mexico, which at that time also included Arizona. Santa Anna indicated this was not unreasonable and advised that the United States seize Saltillo and

Tampico. He also suggested the best way to take Veracruz without having to reduce the great fortress of San Juan de Ulúa in the harbor would be to land south of the city. The wily dictator also gave pledges that he knew would strike a chord with the United States: popular government, reduction of the power and wealth of the church, and free trade. By the time the meeting had concluded, Santa Anna's return to Mexico was simply a matter of time and scheduling.[17]

As it turned out, both Polk and Santa Anna had misread the signs. The overall indifference to Paredes's war effort stemmed not from a desire for peace, but from his administration's fatal loss of prestige in the wake of Arista's defeats at Palo Alto and Resaca de la Palma. The Mexican public was still determined to smash the invaders and drive them from the country. By late July Paredes found his position untenable and handed the government over to Vice President Nicolás Bravo. On August 4 Gen. José Mariano Salas led the Mexico City garrison in declaring for Santa Anna. The Paredes–Bravo government collapsed and Salas assumed the presidency, which everyone knew would simply be an interregnum pending Santa Anna's arrival. The declaration for popular government, however, implied a continuation of the war. When Santa Anna landed in Veracruz twelve days later he found his peace plan thwarted and opted to follow public opinion and emerge as the great war leader who would save the nation.[18] Accordingly, he took command of the army and reorganized it as the "Republican Army of Liberation," a designation that reflected his grasp of the Mexican character and how it was influenced by labels.[19] The word "Liberation" was designed to convince the people that the army stood between them and American enslavement, and "Republican" made him a champion against Paredes and the Monarchists. Thus, Santa Anna believed he could neutralize all enemies, foreign and domestic. By the time he reached Mexico City on September 15, he was totally committed to war.[20]

On the Rio Grande, Taylor continued his preparations for the move against Monterrey. The Rangers had already scouted within eighty miles of the city and determined Camargo was the best

Texas Ranger Capt. Ben McCulloch, seated, center, interrogates a Mexican deserter. Rangers, many of whom spoke Spanish and knew the country, proved invaluable to Taylor in gathering information on enemy strength, and the best routes into the Mexican interior. *John Frost,* Pictorial History of Mexico and the Mexican War *(Philadelphia: Charles Desilver, 1862), Author's Collection.*

route. It was only about 150 miles from Monterrey and the troops could be supplied by steamers coming upriver from Brazos Santiago and Matamoros.[21] His plans were disrupted, however, when the Comanches began raiding along the Rio Grande between Camargo and Laredo. On July 22 the troops in Camargo learned that a large party under the war chief Buffalo Hump was raiding ranches on both sides of the river, stealing livestock, murdering men, and carrying off women.[22]

Taylor ordered General Worth, who had recovered from his chagrin, returned to Texas, and was now in command at Camargo, to make certain the area around Mier was secure from the Comanches. "I deem it a paramount duty to protect the Mexican citizens from their ravages, and to apprehend and punish them if possible," Taylor wrote to Adjutant General Jones in

Washington. "Should we exhibit any lukewarmness in this matter, the cry would instantly be raised that the Indians are our allies— an impression already carefully disseminated by the Mexican [political] chiefs."[23]

Worth sent a company of Rangers under Capt. Ben McCulloch, which crossed the Rio Grande at Davis's landing (now Rio Grande City), and followed the river trail up through a series of ranches that were deserted because tenants had fled the Indians Several Mexicans who were questioned described the raids and the routes the Indians had taken. Farther along, they came to a ranch where the Comanches had killed the cattle, stolen horses, and captured young woman and several children. They also learned that the Indians had crossed the river, so they crossed also and went to Mier to requisition rations. Several of the Rangers were survivors of the Mier expedition and one, Lt. John McMullen, gave an impromptu tour covering important scenes of the fight. The veterans were more nostalgic than bitter, the people were friendly, and the stay was pleasant. Meanwhile, McCulloch learned that the Comanches had turned back toward the north-west, making further pursuit pointless. He turned his company back to Camargo.[24]

Taylor arrived in Camargo on August 8. He was gathering information on the best roads to Monterrey and expected to depart no later than September 1. He estimated his force at about six thousand men, of which 3,200 would be regular soldiers. Turning his attention to the overall theater of operations, he sent instructions to Brig. Gen. John E. Wool in San Antonio to march southwest and capture Chihuahua. In mid-August he started Worth toward Cerralvo, about midway between Camargo and Monterrey, and by late that month the U.S. vanguard occupied the town. The Monterrey campaign had begun.[25]

6.
MONTERREY

AS TAYLOR MOVED AGAINST MONTERREY, Polk wrestled with the problems of heading a nation at war. Although the halls of Congress might echo with anti-war talk, the American people greeted the conflict with unbridled enthusiasm, and there had been little problem raising volunteers. Nevertheless, dissent remained. The war accelerated the national debt, adding a tremendous burden to a government that only recently had been forced to enact an unpopular tariff in order to ease its financial problems. The country was divided not only between sectional interests, but by the continuing animosity between nativists and Protestants on the one hand, and immigrants and Roman Catholics on the other. Northern abolitionists stepped up their complaint that the war's primary aim was to expand Southern slavery. While most were Whigs, the occasional Democrat added his voice to the outcry. Perhaps the most notable was Rep. David Wilmot of Pennsylvania, initially a Polk Democrat, who became increasingly uneasy about the president's policies. In August, as Congress considered a war appropriation bill, Wilmot introduced an amendment drafted by an Ohio abolitionist. Assuming that new territory would be acquired from Mexico at the end of the war, the amendment, known to history as the Wilmot Proviso, proposed to prohibit the extension of slavery into this territory. Although the Wilmot Proviso ultimately was defeated, the debate carried into the next session of Congress, deepening the divisions between parties and regions, as well as boosting feeling against the war.[1]

James Russell Lowell, a Boston poet, abolitionist, and literary critic, expressed the position of many. Lowell was outraged when Massachusetts Gov. George Briggs, a Whig, called for ten companies of volunteer troops in response to Polk's levy, and when Edward Webster, son of vehement abolitionist Sen. Daniel Webster, offered to organize and lead one of the companies.[2]

Writing under the pseudonym of Hosea Biglow, whom he represented as a plain, but shrewd Yankee farmer, Lowell condemned not only the war, but also the whole concept of Manifest Destiny. In acquiescing to the "Southern slave conspiracy," Lowell contended that "Yankee renegaders" were forfeiting their own liberty. Commenting on his state's participation, he wrote:

Massachusetts, God forgive her,
She's akneelin' with the rest,
She, thet ough' to ha' clung fer ever
In her grand old eagle-nest;
She thet ough' to stand so fearless
Wile the wracks [rocks] are round her hurled,
Holdin' up a beacon peerless
To the oppressed of all the world. . . .
Let our dear old Bay State proudly
Put the trumpet to her mouth,
Let her ring this messidge loudly
In the ears of all the South:—
"I'll return ye good fer evil
Much ez we frail mortils can
But I wun't go help the Devil
Makin' man the cus o' man;
Call me coward, call me traiter,
Jest ez suits your mean idees,
Here I stand a tyrant-hater,
An' the friend o' God an' Peace!"[3]

The Biglow poems, which appeared in the Boston newspapers, struck a dormant chord in New Englanders, who gave them a wide and popular reception. Two years later they were collected and published as *The Biglow Papers* under the fictitious editorship of one "Homer Wilbur," another of Lowell's literary creations.[4]

Yet for all the allegations of a slave conspiracy, one of the Senate's most vocal opponents of the war was also one of the most vocal supporters of the "Southern slaveocracy," John C. Calhoun of South Carolina. Although Calhoun's views undoubtedly were influenced by a desire to seek the presidency in 1848, and therefore the need to appease northern opposition, he did raise very serious and prophetic questions about the president's nearly unrestrained constitutional powers as commander-in-chief of the armed forces. Although there had been "hostilities," Calhoun maintained, actual war did not exist and could not be prosecuted unless and until declared by Congress. By allowing Polk to provoke a war and then accepting it as a *fait accompli*, Congress had abdicated its responsibilities to serve as a check on executive power.

"It sets the example," he wrote, "which will enable future Presidents to bring about a state of things, in which Congress shall be forced, without deliberation, or reflection, to declare war, however opposed to its convictions of justice or expediency."[85] Similar arguments would be raised again more than a century later in the large-scale, undeclared, conflicts in Korea and Vietnam.

While politicians and dissidents argued over the justice of the war, General Taylor's troops were on the march. Their goal, Monterrey, is the gateway for any army wanting to penetrate Mexico from the north. Situated in a pass in the Sierra Madre Oriental, it guards a broad valley that leads hundreds of miles south into the Mexican interior. In 1846 the city's main defense was the Citadel, a large fortress whose forbidding appearance led the Americans to dub it the "Black Fort." Two additional forts, the Tenería (Tannery) and the Diablo (Devil) covered either side of the road by which the U.S. forces would approach. On the opposite site of the city were two fortified heights, Independence Hill and Federation Hill. These commanded the entire city and protected the road from Saltillo in the west, from which any Mexican reinforcements might be expected to come. Monterrey itself was laid out around a main plaza, with streets extending out at right angles to each other. The buildings along these streets were built of solid stone with flat roofs, making each a potential fort. The advantages were apparent to General Ampudia, who had been reinstated after Arista's disasters on the Rio Grande, and he fortified every strong point, connecting them all with temporary barricades. But the very strength of Monterrey was its weakness. With so many heavy defenses, the units were too far apart to support each other; thus, each fortified point could be cut off from support and reduced individually.[6]

The first U.S. units began marching out of Cerralvo on September 12. The army moved in sections at one-day intervals. Taylor and his staff accompanied the First Division under General Twiggs, which left at daybreak on September 13. The fighting spirit was high. The Texans, all of whom were mounted, went by way of China, on the Reynosa Road, while the main army took the main road from Cerralvo. Taylor expected them to come together at Marín, twenty-four miles from Monterrey. Ironically, Ampudia had inspected Marín on September 11, and on the advice of his engineers, had determined to stop Taylor there. However, he could not persuade his nervous generals, who had no more confidence in his abilities in Monterrey than they had in Matamoros. Additionally, many of his soldiers had fought at Palo Alto and Resaca de la Palma and morale was as low among Ampudia's troops as it was high among Taylor's.[7]

If Ampudia was a poor general, he was a prolific writer. He issued proclamations warning Mexicans and foreign citizens against aiding the enemy or trafficking in contraband under penalty of death. Others, printed in English, urged U.S. soldiers to surrender, promising safe conduct to the interior of Mexico. These were scattered along the roads and found their way into the U.S. camps as the army drew closer to Marín. Despite the overall morale, the proclamation had some effect. Several foreign-born soldiers, as well as disgruntled native-born Americans, did desert, joining those who had gone over on the Rio Grande to serve in the Mexican army at Monterrey. Organized into an artillery unit by John Riley, an Irish-born deserter, they formed the nucleus of Mexico's myth-shrouded San Patricio Battalion.[8]

The U.S. forces came together at Marín on September 18 and the army marched out early the next morning. Lt. Dilworth wrote in his diary, "As the Dragoons passed us, [Second Lt. Delos] Sackett

THEN AND NOW

Mexico's preservation efforts are directed primarily at pre-Columbian sites and outstanding examples of colonial history and architecture. Consequently, battlefields do not have a significant priority, and Mexican War sites that have been developed are those that have historic or cultural significance extending beyond the war, such as the Bishop's Palace in Monterrey, or Chapúltepec, Molino del Rey, and Churubusco, in Mexico City. Interestingly enough, many of the sites in the northern part of the country remain reasonably close to their appearance at the time of the war, although there is little, if any, attempt to designate them as historic sites or relate them to the conflict.

One can follow the course of the war in northern Mexico generally along two federal highways, M 2 and M 54. Neither Matamoros nor Reynosa, both modern cities, retain much from the early nineteenth century. The one significant Mexican War site in Matamoros is the Casa Mata, a fortín or blockhouse, constructed as part of the city's defenses in the early 1840s. Located on Degollado Street at its intersection with República de Guatemala Street, it was restored in the late 1960s and is now a regional historical museum.

Camargo, directly across from Rio Grande City, Texas, may be reached either by M 2 from Reynosa, or by crossing the bridge at Rio Grande City. The area around the main square is little changed from the period of U.S. occupation in 1846 and the Church of Santa Ana de Camargo on the square appears much as it did in contemporary sketches.

Highway M 54 begins in Ciudad Miguel Alemán, opposite Roma, Texas, and essentially follows Taylor's route through Mier, Cerralvo, Monterrey, and Saltillo to Buena Vista. Except for modern traffic improvements and the atrocious Victorian clock tower mounted on one corner of the eighteenth-century church, Mier is little changed from when the Texans fought there in 1842 and when the U.S. forces occupied it during the war. The same may be said for Cerralvo.

asked me if I heard the 'Elephant' groan in Monterrey."[9] This was Dilworth's last entry; he was mortally wounded when a cannonball tore off his leg two days later.[10]

After a day's march, the troops arrived at a hacienda a few miles from Monterrey and established a camp in a grove of trees that the Americans dubbed "Walnut Springs." On September 19 Taylor accompanied the two Texas regiments to the edge of the city to reconnoiter. About 9 A.M. they emerged on a broad plain as the morning haze lifted to reveal the massive Citadel only two miles away. Suddenly, a gun fired from the fortress, and a cannonball bounced along the ground nearby. More volleys followed. Excited at the prospect of a fight, and eager to challenge the enemy, the Texans galloped toward the Citadel, zigzagging to avoid the shot, and defying the frustrated Mexican gunners, who could not shift their pieces rapidly enough to compensate for range or direction.[11]

Watching the performance, James K. Holland of Wood's Regiment wrote

Many of their balls were directed very well—yet no one was hurt. It was cheering to see how The Texians greeted the Mexican Balls—Every fire was met with a hearty response of 3 cheers and such waving of hats and huzzaing Genl T[.] says he never heard—The Texians proved their spunk by the utter carelessness with which the[y] Rec[eive]d the Enemy's shot—They whizzing by us in all directions.[12]

At 4 P.M. Taylor sent Mansfield with the engineers and an escort of Texas Rangers to have a better look at the city. The detachment was gone for six hours, much of which was spent under heavy fire. Mansfield determined that the key to Monterrey was the Bishop's Palace, which was located on a spur of Independence Hill overlooking the city from the west and commanding the whole with its guns. The building was constructed in 1787 as the Palace of Nuestra Señora de Guadalupe for Dr. Rafael José Verger y Suau, bishop of Nuevo León. Less a palace than a strongly built mansion, it was a retreat for the bishop and a refuge from the summer heat. The strategic location of the palace was recognized during the Mexican War of Independence, and in 1816 Royalist forces converted it into an artillery post to defend Monterrey against insurgents. From that time on, it served primarily as a military installation.[813]

Although the palace itself was heavily fortified, the western defenses otherwise were relatively weak. Once the palace batteries were in U.S. hands and turned against the city, Taylor believed Monterrey might surrender without further resistance. If, however, the entire army tried to skirt the city and come in

The Bishop's Palace in Monterrey, shown in a contemporary drawing, above, and a modern photograph, below. Except for the addition of the cupola in the 1850s and the late-twentieth-century reconstruction of the colonial-era arcades, the building appears much as it did at the time of the war. Despite modern landscaping and terracing, the visitor still realizes the formidable nature of the building and the difficulty in climbing the hill to take it. Top, *John Frost,* Pictorial History of Mexico and the Mexican War *(Philadelphia: Charles Desilver, 1862), Author's Collection.* Bottom, *Author's Photo.*

against Independence Hill from the west, the rear would be exposed to fire from the Citadel. Consequently, he made a decision that, for him, was totally uncharacteristic—he divided the army. Worth would take part of the troops, circle around north of Monterrey, and come in from the west, cutting the Saltillo road and moving against the palace and the batteries across the valley on Federation Hill. The main body of troops then would move in from the east, between the forts of Tenería and Diablo, cutting them off from each other and entering the city through the middle. The problem was that Taylor essentially was an infantry officer who had made his career as an Indian fighter. He had never been up against true military fortifications planned and constructed by trained engineers. He appeared to have only marginally understood that his light field artillery would be useless against the heavy walls and had misplaced confidence in the musket and bayonet. These failings would prove costly in the battle that followed.

The battle of Monterrey began at 2 P.M. on September 20 when Worth's division, with Jack Hays and the First Texas Mounted Rifles in the lead, began moving north. To distract the Mexicans, Taylor moved the remainder of the army out onto the plain and began a bombardment of the eastern defenses. Unfortunately, his guns did little more than make noise. Correctly guessing Taylor's intentions, Ampudia rushed more troops to Independence Hill and sent General Torrejón's cavalry to hold the Saltillo road. Worth's men found the terrain more difficult than they had originally believed. Part of it was dense brush and pioneers had to hack a path for the cavalry and artillery. Then they came into fields of cane and corn where the ground was soft. As the day drew to a close they had covered only seven miles, and Worth ordered the men into camp just beyond the range of the guns at the Bishop's Palace. Then he rode ahead with Hays and the Texans, who encountered a detachment of Mexican cavalry. In the ensuing fight, the Mexicans were decoyed into a cornfield where dismounted Texans concealed among the stalks fired at point-blank range. The palace batteries opened up with shell, and the explosions panicked the mounted Texans' horses. Everyone began milling about in confusion, and Worth and the Texans took advantage of nightfall to retreat to their camp.

After a cold, rainy night without shelter, Worth's men moved out about sunrise and soon collided with about two hundred Mexican cavalry. The Texans, who were in the lead, took shelter behind a wall and opened fire, with two batteries of U.S. artillery joining in. The Mexicans scattered and by 8:15 A.M. Worth had cut the road to Saltillo. From there, he decided to move against the fortifications on Federation Hill. Three hundred infantrymen and dismounted Texans forded the Santa Catarina River and began moving up the hill, while the rest of the troops fended off Torrejón's cavalry's efforts to cut them off. More infantry units were sent to reinforce the initial group and soon the guns of Federation Hill were in U.S. hands and turned against the batteries on Independence Hill.

Elsewhere, the situation was not going as well. Unable to decide on a specific plan, Taylor sent his troops piecemeal into the city to take the Diablo and the Tenería. The U.S. troops stormed into the narrow streets, only be forced back by a galling fire from the fortified houses. The Tenería fell, but lack of artillery support forced the troops assaulting the Diablo to withdraw. Aside from Worth's victory on the Saltillo Road, the only thing accomplished was the capture of the Tenería, but at the cost of 394 casualties.[14]

Going once again into a cold, rainy camp, Worth determined to move on Independence Hill and the palace. His troops began moving out at 3 A.M. with Hays's Texans in the lead. Rangers Addison Gillespie and W. W. (Bigfoot) Wallace took advantage of the morning fog to scout up close to the base of the hill. While they reconnoitered, the fog lifted and a Mexican sentry fired on them, mortally wounding Gillespie in the abdomen. Wallace carried him to the rear.

The main body of Texans was almost to the hill when they encountered Mexican infantry and cavalry. Hays deployed his men as skirmishers while U.S. infantry and artillery came up from behind. The first of the Independence defenses, Libertad, fell about dawn, and a 12-pound howitzer was dragged up in pieces and reassembled to bombard the Bishop's Palace. Meanwhile,

A contemporary drawing shows a Texas Ranger of the Mexican War, with his typical wide-brimmed hat and his preferred weapons, a long rifle and a heavy Bowie knife. The saddle appears to be a variant of the U.S. military issue. The Western-style saddle had not yet been developed from its Mexican ancestry. *John Frost,* Pictorial History of Mexico and the Mexican War *(Philadelphia: Charles Desilver, 1862), Author's Collection.*

units of the Fifth and Seventh U.S. Infantry Regiments deployed to catch any Mexican counterattack in a vicious crossfire. The howitzer soon silenced the palace batteries, making the Mexican position untenable. They attacked, but were driven back by the crossfire, with U.S. infantrymen hard on their heels. The two sides were so close that soldiers of both armies were scrambling over the palace walls at the same time. The Mexicans fought desperately as the Americans forced their way into the building. In the great hall, fighting was hand-to-hand. Finally, the Mexican defenders had enough and the palace was surrendered.[15]

General Taylor, meanwhile, had recovered his decisiveness, while General Ampudia had lost his. Despite the loss of the Tenería and Independence and Federation Hills, Ampudia's position was still strong and the outcome of the battle was by no means certain. Nevertheless, about midnight he decided to abandon all the outer defenses except the Citadel and to concentrate his forces around the main square, an action that infuriated the Mexican soldiers who had fought so hard to hold those positions. Nevertheless, they obeyed and prepared for house-to-house fighting.

On September 23, in the midst of a thunderstorm, the veterans of Wood's Second Texas led the assault into the center of town. The determination of the dismounted Rangers, running up the streets in pouring rain and dodging bullets from the rooftops, star-tled both the American regulars and the Mexican defenders. The Texans took some of the houses, driving out the Mexican defend-ers, and used crowbars and sledge hammers to punch holes in the stone walls to move from one house to the next.[16]

"Often there was only a single wall between the Texans and Mexicans," Ranger James Buckner (Buck) Barry wrote, "so as soon as the Texans battered a hole through the wall the Mexicans would commence shooting at random through it. It was nothing strange for the muzzles of the Texans' and Mexicans' guns to clash together, both intending to shoot through the hole at the same time."[17]

"Every house was a castle and filled with soldiers," Upton wrote to his family. "The riflemen soon made them clear as fast as they could. They all retreated to the neighborhood of the plaza, or publick square. Stores and houses were broken open, and I sup-pose the Volunteers made some big raises."[18]

By 11 P.M. the troops were nearing the plaza, supported by a mortar that threw shell into the square. At 2 P.M. on September 24 Taylor ordered U.S. forces to withdraw so that he could bombard the city. Now it was the Texans' turn to be furious. The fall of the city was certain and they believed it was senseless to give up now. They remained in place, hunkering down to avoid the exploding shells, and, amazingly, no one was hurt.[19]

If the fall of the city was obvious to the Texans, it was also obvi-ous to the Mexicans. That night, Nuevo León Gov. Francisco Morales sought a U.S. safe-conduct to evacuate the city, and the next day, September 24, General Ampudia offered to surrender the city provided he was allowed to withdraw his army intact. Taylor appointed a commission consisting of Worth, Texas gover-nor and Maj. Gen. J. Pinckney Henderson, and his former son-in-law, Col. Jefferson Davis. After extensive negotiations, the U.S. commissioners agreed to the Mexican demand to withdraw under arms, and with one six-gun field battery, followed by an eight-week armistice.[20]

Taylor's agreement to allow a Mexican withdrawal has stirred controversy ever since, but his position gave him little option. He only had about five thousand men and the slow, brutal, house-to-house fighting had left them exhausted. He had no siege guns or entrenching tools and therefore would have had to take the Citadel by assault, with heavy losses. Had such an assault been thrown back, he would have been forced to retreat, encumbered by sick and wounded, through a hostile country. Assuming he could have captured the fortress, he did not have enough troops to prevent the Mexican Army from escaping intact, nor did he have the means to pursue it. In any case, Ampudia would have kept his army, but Taylor spared dozens of U.S. lives by allowing Ampudia to evacuate. This also placed the onus of surrender on the Mexicans, undermining their already shaky confidence, while giving his own men a substantial victory.[21]

The Mexican troops withdrew from the city on September 25. Watching them march past, Captain Henry noted:

Several of our deserters were recognized in the ranks of the enemy, the most conspicuous of whom was an Irishman by the name of Riley, who has been appointed a captain in the artillery of the enemy. He was recognized by his old mess-mates, and passed them amid hisses and a broadside of reproaches. The dastard's cheek blanched, and it was with difficulty he retained his position on his gun.[22]

7.
BUENA VISTA

WHILE TAYLOR CONSOLIDATED his position around Monterrey, the buildup of troops and supplies continued along the Rio Grande. A substantial depot had grown up at Brazos Santiago opposite Point Isabel and across the channel from Padre Island. One officer described it as "a few houses, great piles of stores, immense number of wagons and mules and a good deal of business in loading, unloading moving and moving [*sic*] stores, etc." A Mississippi riverboat had been run ashore as a hotel and served "steamboat fare" for twenty dollars a month. The heavy activity was not only to supply Taylor's troops in Monterrey, but also a column under Brig. Gen. John C. Wool, which was marching southwest from San Antonio to Chihuahua. Steamers pushed as far as possible upriver in order to lessen the overland distance to Wool's troops, although beyond Camargo the level of the river was erratic.[1]

The various unfamiliar tropical illnesses continued to plague the troops who were unused to the semi-tropical climate. Col. Samuel Ryan Curtis of the Third Ohio Volunteers, himself only recently recovered from fever, recorded a retreat ceremony in Matamoros on September 24. "The regiment is improving a little in health," he wrote. "This parade was better attended than many have been. Still there is 135 on the sick report for the 8 companies located on this side [of the river]." The following day he commented, "The regiment of Illinois troops are directed to proceed on their way up to Comargo [*sic*]. They leave an additional number of sick. The number in the public hospitals, not including my sick who are in camp, are said to be 800!" And on September 29 he added, "Our army in fact [is] daily diminishing by sickness and death."[2]

News of the fall of Monterrey, which arrived that same day, did little to brighten spirits. The report of some five hundred casualties, weighed against the meager overall strength of the army, was depressing. Added to that was the fact that the Mexicans had evacuated the city intact and under arms, and it seemed that the victory might be frittered away. Besides groundless rumors that a large Mexican force was marching on Matamoros, the troops had to deal with real harassment from Mexican irregulars. Nevertheless, the victory at Monterrey was celebrated by salutes fired by the batteries at Fort Brown, and by U.S. troops occupying Fort Paredes in Matamoros.[3]

The news, likewise, brought no joy in Washington. President Polk and cabinet, sitting at their desks, believed that Taylor had lost an opportunity to end the war by allowing the Mexican Army to evacuate. On October 12, the day after Taylor's dispatches arrived, the president and cabinet unanimously agreed to order him to "terminate the armistice to which he agreed, and to prosecute the war with energy and vigor."[4]

Taylor, meanwhile, had problems of his own. On October 5 a soldier named Fitzsimmons, part of Jack Hays's First Texas Volunteers, was accused of ambushing and killing a Mexican lancer, who was riding down a street under arms but apparently minding his own business. The Mexicans immediately protested, forcing Taylor to reply that he lacked the appropriate judicial staff for trial and could only place the man in confinement. He did, however, muster out the entire force of Texas volunteers, reporting to the adjutant general that, "With their departure we may look for a restoration of quiet and order in Monterey . . . some shameful atrocities have been perpetrated by them since the capitulation of the town."[5]

Taylor was also concerned about General Ampudia, who had withdrawn to Saltillo, some fifty miles to the southwest, in hopes of fortifying the city and making a stand. This proved impractical, however, because the Mexicans would have had to fortify five points over a line of defense totaling about sixty-five miles. In the

THEN AND NOW

Monterrey may be reached either from Reynosa, or by crossing the border at either Rio Grande City/Camargo or Roma/Miguel Alemán and following Taylor's route. Highway M 2 follows the river from Camargo to Miguel Alemán, and from there M 54 goes through Mier, Cerralvo, and Monterrey. The city is dominated by the Cerro de la Silla (Saddle Mountain), which appears in Mexican War-era artwork, as well as on the modern Nuevo León automobile license plates. The third-largest city in Mexico, Monterrey has grown up around the Bishop's Palace, which may be reached from the through-town Gonzalitos freeway (Museo Obispado exit) or from Hidalgo Street downtown. Extensively restored over a forty-year period beginning in 1956, it is cited as the only eighteenth-century monument in Monterrey and a symbol of the city's colonial heritage. It is now a museum of the region from pre-Columbian to modern times. Although the hill has been terraced and landscaped and is surrounded by development, a visitor nevertheless gets a sense of the struggle U.S. forces faced to reach the palace. There is some mention of the Mexican War, although as only one of many historic events involving the palace. Also significant are personal items belonging to Bernardo Gutiérrez de Lara, who was active in Texas in 1812–1814 during the Mexican independence movement. The site of the Citadel (Black Fort) is at Juárez and Tapia Streets downtown. Part of the original structure exists as a theater.

Just south of Saltillo on M 54, a monument marks the site of the battle of Buena Vista, known in Mexico as Angostura. Despite a cement plant off to one side, and some agriculture and orchards, the battlefield is well preserved, although there have been no serious efforts to develop it as a historic site.

wake of Monterrey, Ampudia had neither men nor artillery for such a feat. Additionally, both he and General Santa Anna suspected a U.S. advance against San Luis Potosí. Consequently, Santa Anna ordered Ampudia to concentrate his forces around the latter city, where he relieved Ampudia and personally took command of the army. His suspicions appeared confirmed when he received formal notification from General Taylor, written under orders from Washington, that hostilities would resume on November 13.[6]

One day before the armistice expired, Taylor accompanied General Worth, with about a thousand men and a battery of artillery toward Saltillo, arriving on November 16. Despite Santa Anna's reasonable fears, he had no intention of advancing beyond there, because he lacked the troops he felt were necessary for a thrust deep into the heartland of Mexico. Additionally, much of the three hundred miles between Saltillo and San Luis Potosí was arid, with little chance of obtaining water or supplies, particularly for one unfamiliar with the country. Saltillo, on the other hand, was close, undefended, and separated the interior of Mexico from both Monterrey on the east and the rich farming district around Parras immediately to the west.

General Wool, meanwhile, had reached Monclova and found the direct route to Chihuahua to be waterless. Besides, he could not see any advantage to occupying Chihuahua when the United States already controlled Santa Fe, New Mexico, to the northwest, and Saltillo to the southeast. Taylor agreed, and ordered him to reprovision in Monclova, then move on to Saltillo.[7] In Victoria, Captain Henry observed:

The impression of some respectable Mexicans at this place is, that there is no chance of peace without another battle; that they must be whipped—whipped soundly—*sacrificed in numbers*, and then they will treat. They say truly that we have not yet seen Mexico—have not touched upon the populous parts—nor associated with *the* people. The latter do not believe they *ever have been beaten;* their pride makes them think it is utterly impossible to vanquish their army . . . that Arista sold them on the 8th and 9th of May! and that Ampudia's cowardice caused the surrender of Monterey! No! they will *not* believe it until a battle is fought in which their loss will be very great.[8]

Henry was correct. In San Luis Potosí, Santa Anna had worked one of the miracles for which he was famous—conjuring an entirely new army out of defeated remnants. Cajoling money from the federal and state governments and from the church, expropriating property, and pledging his own funds, he managed to build a force of twenty-five thousand men. His intelligence service had determined that Wool had been left in Saltillo with only a thousand men

and six pieces of artillery. On December 22 he announced his decision to make a forced march on Saltillo and Monterrey with nine
thousand infantry, four thousand cavalry, and twelve pieces of
artillery. At the same time, Maj. Gen. Gabriel Valencia would take
fifteen hundred cavalry and move against Taylor in Victoria.
Although it took almost a month to put his plan into motion, word
of it reached General Worth, now commanding in Saltillo, and set
off a series of alarms that caused a nearly continuous redeploy-
ment of the U.S. forces between Saltillo, Monterrey, Victoria, and
Camargo, which prompted Santa Anna to cancel his plans.[9]

Meanwhile, the War Department's instructions to Taylor were
ambiguous. President Polk preferred that Taylor not venture
beyond Monterrey, and on October 22 Secretary Marcy advised
against any further movement unless Taylor had "an adequate
force." At the same time, however, Marcy told him to exercise his
own discretion on any movement beyond Monterrey and to
always let the Mexicans believe he was preparing a new offensive.
A new complication arose in December, when Taylor learned he
would be stripped of the bulk of his regular troops and left "to the
defensive" with volunteers. The source of this dilemma was Polk,
who had determined that the war would end only if the United
States occupied Veracruz and from there moved against Mexico
City. Still disappointed with Taylor's conduct at Monterrey, Polk
put aside his earlier animosity toward General Scott and ordered
the general-in-chief to personally handle the expedition. Scott
believed he would have to occupy Veracruz and move inland no
later than the end of March 1847, before the onset of the yellow
fever season on the coast. Not having time to assemble all the men
he believed necessary, and transport them from the United States,
he decided he would have to draw on Taylor's troops.
Accordingly, he advised Taylor that he would need Worth with
up to four thousand regular infantry, along with two field batteries, and five hundred regular cavalry. This would leave Taylor
with sufficient force to defend Monterrey and maintain communications with Camargo and Point Isabel, but little more.[10] Yet, as
one contemporary account states, "With this comparatively small
force, General Taylor not only maintained all the posts within his

command, but with the one half of it achieved the memorable victory at Buena Vista."[11]

Santa Anna, meanwhile, had to move soon because the Mexico City newspapers were attacking his inaction. Fate intervened on his behalf when a U.S. courier, Lt. John A. Richey, was ambushed and killed and his dispatches forwarded to San Luis Potosí. Among the papers were General Scott's instructions to Taylor, detailing the forces being drawn from the north. Given this information, Santa Anna now decided to silence his critics by reviving the Saltillo offensive. He hoped to strike a decisive blow against Taylor's reduced force, retake the northern cities, and drive the United States out of Mexico.

On January 27, the vanguard of the 21,553-man Mexican army marched out of San Luis Potosí and headed north. Over the next several days the rest of the troops followed until Santa Anna himself departed on February 2. The plan was straightforward and practical. Scott's draw on Taylor had reduced his forces to such an extent that his control of the country beyond the population centers was tenuous at best. Even the Mexican cities were held with substantially reduced garrisons. Santa Anna's troops would make a forced march and retake Saltillo, where they would rest and reprovision. A large cavalry force under Brig. Gen. José Vicente Miñón would keep Taylor occupied around Monterrey until Santa Anna's troops arrived. Meanwhile, an army under Maj. Gen. José Urrea would retake Victoria and cut off Taylor's retreat. Guerrillas attached to Urrea's forces were already harassing U.S. communications between Monterrey and Camargo and along the Rio Grande. The main body of American troops then would be bottled up in Monterrey and starved into surrender. Thus, Mexico would retake its northern departments, then turn against Scott on the Gulf Coast. The only problem with the plan was the largely barren, arid march north from San Luis Potosí. If anything prevented Santa Anna from reaching food and water in Saltillo, his army would be finished. Likewise, he knew that if he were defeated and thrown back en route, the army would suffer heavy losses retreating over these wastes. In that case, his own prestige would be severely, perhaps irreparably, damaged.[12]

An unusually accurate nine-teenth-century American draw-ing shows Maj. Gen. Antonio Lopez de Santa Anna wearing the wide-brimmed, tightly woven palm fiber hat of his native Veracruz. Although a dandy on parade, Santa Anna often dressed more practically for field service, eschewing the ornate felt chapeau prescribed by Mexican army regulations in favor of more comfortable head-gear. The artist, who may have been unfamiliar with Mexican military horse equipment, chose to show Santa Anna with a U.S. Army Grimsley saddle fitted with heavy, more Mexican style stirrup hoods. *Author's Collection.*

In Monterrey, Taylor surmised that Richey's dispatches had reached Santa Anna, with the obvious conclusion being that the Mexicans were mounting an offensive against his reduced force. Despite his ill feelings toward the Texans, he was in no position to be selective about troops. Consequently, Taylor summoned the old Mounted Volunteer companies of Rangers from Corpus Christi, along with recently formed units from San Antonio, which brought a particularly dangerous element. One of the new compa-nies called itself the "Mustang Grays" after its commander, Mabry "Mustang" Gray, a vicious cutthroat notorious for robbing and murdering Mexican traders operating out of the Nueces Strip. Another company, headed by Walter P. Lane, was little better. One of Lane's Rangers, John Glanton, was an amiable but brutal sociopath, who later made a career of collecting Indian scalps for the bounty offered by various Mexican jurisdictions.[13]

False alarms about the approaching Mexican army were becom-ing an almost daily occurrence. Adding to Taylor's problems, the

Volunteers not only were unruly among the civilian populace, but were haphazard in performing of their duties. After the Rangers clashed with a group of Mexicans at the fortified hacienda of Encarnación, about fifty-five miles south of Saltillo, separate scouting expeditions sent by General Wool in Saltillo and Maj. Gen. William Butler in Monterrey came together and went into camp at Encarnación. Not bothering to throw out pickets, they found themselves surrounded by five hundred of General Miñón's lancers and were forced to surrender. A relief force of five companies of Arkansas troops under Col. Archibald Yell rode south with a total disregard of caution, only to rush back to Saltillo upon learning that Miñón was nearby with three thousand lancers. Another scouting expedition, consisting of Kentucky troops under Capt. William J. Heady, also was captured. Wool was convinced that a powerful Mexican force was approaching, and at his suggestion Taylor shifted his headquarters from Monterrey to Saltillo, bringing his reserves. In order to keep his Volunteers busy and rebuild their confidence, Taylor moved them out to Agua Nueva, some eighteen miles south of Saltillo, establishing his headquarters there on February 5.

Agua Nueva was on the San Luis Potosí road. To reach it, Taylor had to pass the hacienda of Buena Vista, where Wool already had established headquarters, and go through a defile between the mountains that the Mexicans called Angostura, or the Narrows. Taylor was willing to fight at Agua Nueva. Wool, however, had already scouted Angostura and determined that it could be held with Taylor's relatively small force, whereas Agua Nueva was on an open plain where the U.S. troops could be outflanked on either side. After hearing Wool's argument, Taylor agreed, adding his own reasons: if Santa Anna believed Taylor was retreating from Agua Nueva, he would push his already exhausted, hungry troops that much harder across the desert to catch up and finish the U.S. forces. The stand, then, would be at Angostura, near Hacienda Buena Vista.[14]

On February 20, Col. Charles May took virtually all of the U.S. mounted forces to Encarnación, prepared the hacienda for defense, and was going into camp when a body of Miñón's cavalry appeared. Realizing that Santa Anna would not be far behind, and that Taylor could not afford to be cut off from his cavalry, May withdrew back to Agua Nueva. Arriving at Encarnación the following morning, Santa Anna reviewed his troops and ordered Masses celebrated for the various divisions. The brutal march north, during which the poorly clad and equipped soldiers suffered alternately from heat and cold, as well as from hunger and thirst, had cost the army four thousand men from death, illness, or desertion. With the prospect of battle drawing close, however, those still capable of fighting showed renewed enthusiasm. Santa Anna detached Miñón, sending him on a secondary road toward Saltillo, while he marched the bulk of the army along the main road toward Agua Nueva. He did not notice a party of Texans under Maj. Ben McCulloch that was shadowing him. The Texans followed long enough to form a good idea about the size of the Mexican force, which McCulloch estimated in excess of twenty thousand. With this information, Taylor followed his plan and withdrew to Buena Vista at noon on February 21. Knowing Wool was capable of organizing a defense at Angostura, Taylor continued on to Saltillo. Although not aware that Miñón was moving north on a secondary road, he realized that there were many such roads, and wanted to ascertain that his rear was secure. That done, he rode the six miles back to Buena Vista on February 22.[15]

Soon after Taylor arrived, he was approached by a Mexican truce team with a letter from Santa Anna, who was now at Encantada, only a few miles to the south. The Mexican general wrote:

You are surrounded by twenty thousand men, and cannot, in any human probability, avoid suffering a route, and being cut to pieces with your troops; but as you deserve consideration and particular esteem, I wish to save you from a catastrophe, and for that purpose give you this notice, in order that you may surrender at discretion, under the assurance that you will be treated with the consideration belonging to the Mexican character, to which end you will be granted an hour's time to make up your mind, to commence from the moment when my flag of truce arrived in your camp.

With this view, I assure you of my particular consideration.[16]

Samuel Chamberlain, a Volunteer serving under General Wool, later wrote that Taylor told Bliss to "tell Santa Anna to go to hell."[17] The official reply, however, was a single, polite though slightly sarcastic sentence declining Santa Anna's "request."[18]

The Mexican army spent much of the day deploying. The last sixty miles of their march had been particularly exhausting, and some of the soldiers actually had died of fatigue and had been left where they had fallen along the road. Even so, more than fourteen thousand troops were fit for battle, and the mass of soldiers had to be sent into position over rough terrain. The road through which the Mexicans had to pass narrowed down to forty feet, with steep bluffs on the east and steep ravines on the west. The ravines were hard enough for infantry but virtually impassable for artillery and cavalry. Wool had placed one battery at the edge of the ravines, practically on the road itself, protected by units of the First Illinois and the Third Indiana. The remainder of the First Illinois defended the most vulnerable position, a small plateau, about fifty feet high, overlooking the road as it entered the pass, and approached by a ravine about a mile and a half to the east. The Second Indiana, Second Illinois, and Second Kentucky, with an amalgamation of artillery borrowed from the three batteries, formed an oblique line to protect the plateau from the ravine. One last important point was a long narrow ridge beyond the plateau, leading around the U.S. line. Because its configuration did not appear conducive to the movement of an army, Wool initially ignored the ridge. He completely failed to consider a mountain east of the plateau. Santa Anna, however, grasped its possibilities as an artillery emplacement, which might even enable him to outflank Taylor and attack him from the rear. Accordingly, he sent Ampudia's light infantry and a light cavalry brigade under Brig. Gen. Julián Juvera to occupy the height.[19]

The battle of Buena Vista (or Angostura, as it is known in Mexico), began at 3 P.M. on February 22 when a division under Brig. Gen. Santiago Blanco skirmished with the U.S. troops defending the road in the pass. Although nothing came of it, Taylor belatedly noticed Ampudia's men moving up the heights and sent Col. Humphrey Marshall with two complete cavalry regiments and a battalion of infantry to head them off. Sporadic fighting continued all afternoon until Ampudia outflanked Marshall and the U.S. troops withdrew to the base of the mountain. Nevertheless, Taylor was satisfied with his troop dispositions and rode back to Saltillo to ascertain conditions in the rear.

Fighting resumed at 2 A.M. on February 23 when Ampudia's infantry drove the U.S. pickets from the heights. Reinforced near daybreak by two thousand additional men, he then attempted to flank Wool's left and come down on him from the rear. Marshall, reinforced by Yell, began moving back up the mountain, while infantry and artillery in the pass threw back a direct assault from Blanco. Ampudia, however, hit Marshall and Yell, and threw them back in disarray, while a division under Maj. Gen. Francisco Pacheco smashed into the Second Indiana and drove it from the plateau. Although it now appeared Wool was outflanked, the Mexicans moved too rapidly, coming abreast of the still dangerous U.S. artillery. Although the cavalry continued to pursue the Indiana troops and Marshall's men, grapeshot brought the Mexican infantry to a halt about 9 A.M., when Taylor arrived from Saltillo. At the outset, it seemed like he had arrived just in time to witness a defeat; at least Wool thought so, and said as much. Taylor, however, remarked to the effect that he alone would decide when the army had been defeated.[20]

The general sent Jefferson Davis's Mississippi rifles, reinforced by the Third Indiana, to back up the Second Indiana and hold the flank. Davis not only held, but advanced against the Mexican infantry, which was being cut to pieces by the U.S. artillery. Meanwhile, the Mexican lancers had broken through and were heading toward Buena Vista. Taylor sent May with four companies of dragoons and two companies of Arkansas Cavalry, which scattered the lancers. Although the San Patricio Battalion had managed to mount a battery on the mountain, the U.S. mobile artillery minimized its effect.

The Mexicans now approached along the ridge that Wool had neglected. The Mississippi Rifles and Third Indiana, supported by Capt. Braxton Bragg's artillery, went up to meet it. The U.S. troops held their fire until the Mexicans were within eighty yards, then all opened up at once, the grapeshot from Bragg's artillery tearing the Mexican lines to pieces. Watching the scene, Taylor remarked, "A little more grape, Captain Bragg!" The Mississippians then drew their Bowie knives and charged in for a hand-to-hand fight. The Mexicans fled into a ravine, and were saved from further losses by a thunderstorm.[21]

By 1 P.M. the tide of battle had shifted, and now it was the Mexicans who worried about defeat. A truce party came out from the Mexican side, but the Mexicans opened fire when Wool rode out to meet it. It was nothing more than a ruse to allow their battered divisions to withdraw and regroup. Taylor now saw the opportunity to counterattack. His force, however, was not sufficient, and the Mexicans rallied and came up to meet it. The U.S. troops were thrown back, but their artillery again shattered the Mexican infantry. Elsewhere, Miñón's advance on Saltillo had been thrown back by a redoubt established in anticipation of such a move. Soon his cavalry would constitute part of the devastated army that retreated southward, strewing the desert with dead men and animals, many of whom succumbed to hunger and sheer exhaustion. The battle of Buena Vista was over.[22]

The Buena Vista campaign was a classic example of Santa Anna's leadership. A brilliant strategist and planner, he was a poor field commander. His forces outnumbered Taylor's by at least four to one. Had he committed the entire army in massive, simultaneous assaults, he probably could have overwhelmed the U.S. troops by sheer numbers. Instead, he used his troops piecemeal, looking for weaknesses in the U.S. lines, and Taylor's troops shifted back and forth as needed to reinforce those weak points. This meant that the conditions during the battle constantly changed, and neither Santa Anna nor his commanders were capable of responding to those changes. Taylor, on the other hand, gave his officers a general objective, and then trusted them to handle their men as the immediate situation required.[23]

The victory was costly. Taylor lost 267 killed, 456 wounded, and 23 missing. Another 1,500 or so had deserted. Taylor himself noted that losses among the officers were "especially severe," with twenty-eight killed outright. Among the dead were Colonel

Yell and Lt. Col. Henry Clay Jr., whose father, the great Kentucky senator, had opposed the war.[24] The ever-critical President Polk complained in his diary about Taylor's moving to Saltillo and Buena Vista, rather than keeping a purely defensive position in Monterrey as Polk and Scott intended. Taylor, he wrote, "has been constantly blundering into difficulties, but has fought out of them, but with very severe loss."[25] The president—indeed most Americans—seemed incapable of understanding that in war nothing matters but the outcome. Armies routinely suffer heavy losses, and generals must weigh the potential losses against the ultimate objectives, or against the consequences of doing nothing. Had Taylor remained in Monterrey, Santa Anna's plan most likely would have borne fruit, and the United States might even have lost the war. As it was, the Mexican offensive collapsed, and Santa Anna, who had been accepted as a savior, began losing credibility at a time Mexico could least afford it. With Buena Vista, the northern campaign effectively ended, and the center of operations shifted to Scott's move against Veracruz and the city of Mexico.

Now that Santa Anna no longer was a threat, boredom set in, and the list of atrocities against the Mexican populace began to grow. It was aggravated by an active guerrilla campaign waged by the irregular forces attached to General Urrea, which was met with a vicious counterguerrilla campaign. State volunteers generally were more likely to commit atrocities than the disciplined regulars. The Arkansans were perhaps the worst, but in the sheer number of depredations the Texans, who already had a reputation for bloodshed, were the most notorious.[26]

The Mustang Grays descended on Rancho de Guadalupe on the pretext of looking for weapons and hanged twenty-five men, riddling their bodies with bullets. No weapons were found. In response, Col. Antonio Canales, the Mexican guerrilla chief, issued a directive to his commanders telling them to "give no quarter to any Americans whom you may find, or who may present themselves to you, even though they be unarmed."[27]

In another incident, Walter P. Lane's Rangers captured a guerrilla chief named Juan Flores and shot him in Cerralvo following a drumhead court martial. A few nights later John Glanton, of Lane's company, gunned down a man in the town of Magdalena.[28]

Disgusted with these atrocities, Taylor decided to muster out the Texans he had, determined not to accept any more. "There is scarcely a form of crime that has not been reported to me as committed by them," he complained to Adjutant General Jones. "The mounted men of Texas have scarcely made one expedition without unwarrantably killing a Mexican."[29]

8.
TEXANS WITH SCOTT

SAMUEL WALKER MISSED THE BATTLES of Monterrey and Buena Vista. On May 27, 1846, he had been commissioned a captain in the Regiment of Mounted Rifles, although he was not formally mustered out of the Rangers until October 2. Newspaper coverage of the war had made the Texas Rangers into national icons, and Walker was seen as the Ranger *sans pareil*. Shortly after he was mustered out, he reported to Washington, where the government used his popularity for a recruiting drive in Maryland. Once that was completed, he met with Samuel Colt to discuss purchasing weapons. As a Ranger, Walker had used Colt's Paterson revolver with a five-shot cylinder that gave the Texans an edge in Indian fights. Now Colt had the prototype for a vastly improved model and, after testing, Walker enthusiastically endorsed it. This brought Colt a desperately needed government contract, and together the two men worked out final specifications. It fired six .44-caliber balls and, at four pounds nine ounces, was designed to fit a saddle holster. Tooling for the Walker Model, as it was formally designated, began in January 1847, and Texas troops would be the first to receive it.[1]

Besides the weapon's utilitarian function, it also provided a psychological edge. However else they might have felt about the United States, Mexicans had a profound respect for American technology. And in Spanish, the word *revolver* is the root of *revuelta*, which describes any number of convoluted motions. On learning that the Texans were armed with *revolveres*, the Mexicans

Texas Ranger Capt. Samuel H. Walker, shown here in uniform after transferring to the U.S. Mounted Rifles, led scouting and reconnaissance expeditions through Mexican lines between Point Isabel and the Rio Grande. Together with Samuel Colt, he developed the Colt's Walker Model, the first military revolver, which was issued to Texas troops in 1847. Walker was killed that same year in a skirmish at Huamantla in central Mexico. *Texas State Library and Archives Commission.*

began to think that the United States had developed a weapon that could fire around objects, turn corners, go through openings, "and hunt up folks generally."[2]

Aside from its weight, however, the Walker Model had two drawbacks. The least important was the weak spring that held the loading lever in place against the barrel. When fired, the lever tended to drop, jamming the plunger into a chamber opening in the cylinder. More critical were the overly large chambers that allowed the pistol to be overloaded, so that sometimes the cylinder blew apart, killing or seriously injuring the soldier firing the weapon. Nevertheless, the Walker Model was a vast improvement over the earlier five-shot, light caliber Colt's Paterson, and the Texas troops eagerly awaited the first shipment.

Walker returned to duty in May 1847, joining General Scott's forces working their way from Veracruz to Mexico City. Although a regular soldier, many troops still thought of him as a Ranger. Part of this no doubt was due to his reputation, but he also was, at this time, the only important Ranger with Scott's army; the others were at home or with Taylor in the north. Scott's greatest problem was protecting his lines between Veracruz and the interior. Even large supply trains were subjected to ferocious guerrilla attacks, and no courier dared carry dispatches without a mounted escort. Walker's Mounted Rifles, who arrived at the Castle of Perote on the National Highway between Jalapa and Puebla on May 25, were given the job of protecting couriers and waging counterguerrilla warfare. Perote almost certainly brought back memories, because Walker had been imprisoned there following the Mier Expedition. The situation almost certainly was aggravated in September when, after a summer of quarrelling and Walker's accusations of cowardice, his commander, Col. F. N. Wyncoop, ordered Walker confined in the castle. He was released on October 4 by order of Brig. Gen. Joseph Lane. In the meantime, Scott had taken Mexico City, but Santa Anna was laying siege to Puebla at his rear.[3]

By now, the new Colt's revolver named in his honor was ready for service, and he had received a pair from Colt. Writing to his brother, Jonathan, Walker said, "there is not an officer who has seen them but what speaks in the highest terms of them and all of the Cavalry officers are determined to get them if possible." The general issue revolvers had arrived at the depot in Veracruz but were tied up by apparent indifference. Complaining to Jonathan, Walker noted that General Lane was preparing to march on Puebla and break Santa Anna's siege.

I think Santa Anna's race is nearly run. Jack Hays will soon be here with his Regt. of Rangers and I have no doubt that Santa Anna will be in a tight place; if I had my revolving pistols I should feel strong hopes of capturing or killing him. I have written three times to the different officers at Vera Cruz [sic] to forward them and two commands have come up since they arrived at Vera Cruz but I have no hopes of getting them until Jack Hays comes up. I have also made repeated applications to go for them but without success.[4]

Walker's company was one of four mounted units that formed Lane's cavalry wing as his brigade pushed toward Puebla.

Learning of the U.S. approach, Santa Anna decided against resisting in the mountain passes. He withdrew instead to the town of Huamantla, about twenty-five miles east of Puebla and just north of the National Highway, where he hoped to remain concealed until Lane passed. Then he would descend with his troops and attack the American rear. Lane, however, learned of the plan, and on October 8 decided to occupy Huamantla. Around 1 P.M. he sent Walker ahead with the cavalry, but cautioned him to stay close enough for infantry support should he encounter heavy resistance.

Walker approached within three miles of the town, where he surprised the Mexican pickets and pursued them through a dense field of maguey that blocked the view of the main American force. Coming into the plaza, the U.S. troops encountered five hundred Mexican lancers supported by artillery. Ordering a charge, Walker broke the line and drove the gunners from their pieces, but then his own men fragmented as they began chasing after the Mexicans. At that point they were attacked and nearly overwhelmed by a much larger body of Mexican lancers just arriving from Puebla. Walker was killed, but his troops managed to hold. Several tried to man the captured guns, but the Mexican gunners had taken the priming tubes when they fled.

The main body of U.S. troops, meanwhile, heard the firing and rushed in to support the cavalry. An Indiana unit was first to arrive, formed into line, and sent a heavy fire into the Mexican ranks. The Mexicans broke and fled, leaving behind 150 killed and wounded. U.S. losses were thirteen killed, including Walker, and eleven wounded. Furious at the losses, particularly of Walker, whom he liked, Lane turned Huamantla over to the troops for plunder. Then, after remaining there overnight, he continued on to Puebla and relieved the siege. Meanwhile, Santa Anna was relieved of command and ordered to his estates, to await the pleasure of yet another Mexican government.[5]

Jack Hays arrived in Veracruz on October 17 and the Rangers went into camp at Vergara, three miles from the city. On October 19 he drew the first two consignments of revolvers at the Veracruz depot. His adjutant, John Salmon Ford, recalled:

Colt's heavy Walker Model six-shot revolver was named in honor of former Texas Ranger Samuel Walker and issued to Texas troops in 1847. One of the heaviest military handguns ever made, it generally was carried in saddle holsters rather than at the waist and it had a demoralizing effect on the Mexicans. *Enrique E. Guerra Collection.*

Many of the men had not used revolvers. Some of them put the smal end of the conical ball down first. [When loaded thus, a] single fire usually burst the cylinder. Some let the loose powder trail around the cylinder; six shots would be fired at once. One day a "greeny" was in his tent cleaning his pistol. The adjutant advised him to remove the caps. He said he would. In a minute or two a pistol shot was heard. Greeny had shot his own horse in the head and put himself afoot.[6]

On October 26 the second shipment of Colts was delivered to Vergara, and Hays instituted regular target practice. By the end of two weeks the men had become proficient in the new weapon. The Walker Model received one of its first tests during a scouting expedition, when about two hundred guerrillas ambushed Hays and twelve men, hoping to overwhelm them by sheer numbers. The Rangers dismounted, got behind their horses, aimed their rifles across the saddles, and waited. When the guerrillas were about thirty yards away, the Texans fired, bringing down several. Switching to their revolvers, the Rangers opened fire and scattered the guerrillas in general confusion.[7]

On November 2 the Rangers left the coast en route to Mexico City. After several fights with guerrillas they reached Jalapa, where the U.S. troops lined the road and cheered. Hays took two companies on to Puebla to meet with General Lane, while the remainder went into camp outside Jalapa. At some point they acquired two Mexican spies, who informed them enemy troops were in the town of Izúcar de Matamoros. Reaching Puebla, Hays advised Lane, who decided to attack.

The march began on November 23. The following day, the advance guard was attacked in a mountain pass by Mexican lancers and guerrillas. Hearing the firing, Hays took some forty men ahead, charged the lancers with revolvers, and broke their line. The Rangers chased the lancers for about a mile when, coming over the top of a crest, they encountered a line of about a thousand Mexican cavalry. Some of the Rangers wanted to rush the line, but Hays ordered them to fall back to the main body of Lane's troops. As they turned about, however, the entire Mexican line opened fire and then charged. The Rangers reached the head of Lane's column and, recharging their revolvers, turned about and fired. Faced with the revolvers, and with Lane's troops, the lancers turned and fled.[8]

The Rangers arrived in Mexico City on December 6, 1847. Fascinated by their fearsome reputation, crowds of Mexicans gathered. The pistol of one of the Rangers came loose from his holster and fell onto the street, discharging one of the chambers. The ball hit a bystander in the leg, and he claimed the Texans were trying to murder him. Nevertheless, the column continued onto the great plaza of the Zócalo and formed up in the center of the square while Hays went into the National Palace to arrange quarters with the U.S. military authorities.

While they sat on their horses waiting, a street vendor passed with a basket of candies on his head. One of the Rangers motioned him over, took a handful of candy and ate it, and then ate two more handfuls. According to Ford, the Ranger intended to pay, but never got the chance to ask the price because the Mexican, assuming he was being robbed, grabbed a cobblestone and threw it at the Ranger. The Texan drew his revolver and killed the Mexican, starting a general panic among the bystanders. As they rode to their quarters at Calle Doncella 26, another bystander was wounded when a Ranger, frustrated at his balking horse, clubbed it over the head with his revolver, causing the pistol to accidentally discharge. That night, several Texans went to the theater, where a pickpocket stole a handkerchief from one of them. The Ranger yelled in Spanish for the thief to stop, and when the pickpocket kept running, the Ranger fired and killed him.[9]

Mexico City was a dangerous place for Americans. Although the war was drawing to a close, the sullen population did not accept occupation without resistance. At the very least, an American walking down the street alone might be jostled into a gutter, and at worst might be mobbed or knifed. This ended in early 1848, when Ranger Adam Allsens inadvertently ventured into one of the worst districts of the city, where he was cut to pieces by a mob. The Rangers spent the remainder of the day going about their business without speaking of the event. That night, Hays and Capt. W. P. Humphreys heard volley fire from revolvers in the distance. The next day, eighty corpses were sent to the morgue. Six Mexicans were killed in a subsequent incident. The mistreatment and killing of Americans soon stopped. Nevertheless, General Scott thought it prudent to reassign the Rangers outside the city, and they spent the remainder of the war clearing the National Highway of guerrillas and bandits posing as guerrillas.[10]

The Treaty of Guadalupe Hidalgo officially ended the war between nations and permanently fixed the border along the Rio Grande. In Texas, however, the guerrilla conflict that raged back and forth along the Rio Grande and Nueces, already well established by the time of the Mexican War, continued for another sixty years, finally coming to an end in the second decade of the twentieth century.

APPENDIX

U.S. Forts in Texas Named for Mexican War Personalities*

Belknap	Near Graham	Lt. Col. (Bvt. Brig. Gen.) William Goldsmith Belknap (died 1851)
Bliss	El Paso	Capt. (Bvt. Lt. Col.) William Wallace Smith Bliss (died 1853)
Brown	Brownsville	Maj. Jacob Brown (mortally wounded in defense of fort; died May 9, 1846)
Chadbourne	Near Brontë	2d Lt. Theodore Lincoln Chadbourne (killed at Resaca de la Palma, May 9, 1846)
Croghan	Burnet	Col. George Croghan (died 1849)
Duncan	Eagle Pass	Col. James Duncan (died 1849)
Ewell	Lower Nueces	1st Lt. Thomas Ewell (killed at Cerro Gordo, April 18, 1847)
Gates	Gatesville	Capt. (Bvt. Maj.) Collinson Reed Gates (died 1849)
Graham	Near Whitney	Lt. Col. William Montrose Graham (killed at Molino del Rey, September 8, 1847)
Inge	Uvalde	1st Lt. Zebulon Montgomery Pike Inge (killed at Resaca de la Palma, May 9, 1846)
Lincoln	D'Hanis	Capt. George Lincoln (killed at Buena Vista, February 23, 1847)
Martin Scott	Fredericksburg	Maj. (Bvt. Lt. Col.) Martin Scott (killed at Molino del Rey, September 8, 1847)

Mason	Mason	2d Lt. George Thompson Mason (killed in Thornton's Skirmish, April 25, 1846)
McKavett	Near Junction	Capt. Henry McKavett (killed at Monterrey, September 21, 1846)
McIntosh	Laredo	Lt. Col. (Bvt. Col.) James Simmons McIntosh (mortally wounded at Molino del Rey; died September 26, 1847)
Merrill	Upper Nueces	Capt. Moses Emery Merrill (killed at Molino del Rey, September 8, 1847)
Quitman	Upper Rio Grande	Maj. Gen. (Volunteers) John Anthony Quitman (died 1858)
Ringgold	Rio Grande City	Capt. (Bvt. Maj.) Samuel Ringgold (mortally wounded at Palo Alto; died May 11, 1846)
Stockton	Fort Stockton	Cmdre. Robert F. Stockton, USN
Terrett	Near Junction	1st Lt. John Chapman Terrett (killed at Monterrey, September 21, 1846)
Worth	Fort Worth	Col. (Bvt. Maj. Gen.) William Jenkins Worth (died 1849)

* Ranks listed are those held at the time of death or upon leaving the service. Fort Davis is not included here because it was named for Jefferson Davis in his capacity as secretary of war, rather than for his Mexican War service.

NOTES

1. TEXAS, MANIFEST DESTINY, AND NATIONAL HONOR

[1] Ramsey's translation, titled *The Other Side: Or Notes for the History of the War Between the Mexico and the United States, Written in Mexico* (New York: John Wiley, 1850), was compiled by about a dozen Mexican participants who met in Querétaro in 1847 to record their accounts, apparently under the guidance of Ramón Alcaráz, who generally is credited with the work. It was published in Mexico the following year as *Apuntes para la historia de la guerra entre México y los Estados Unidos*. Ramsey kept the Mexican title, adding only "The Other Side" to the beginning, but did not attribute it to Alcaráz or any other particular Mexican author or group of authors. See Seymour V. Connor and Odie B. Faulk, *North America Divided: The Mexican War, 1846–1848* (New York: Oxford University Press, 1971), 206. Neither Jenkins nor Brooks, whose works are among the best contemporary accounts of the war, address the issue of slavery or expansionism. Brooks, representing the Whig point of view, contends that Polk provoked the war by sending Taylor to the Rio Grande. Jenkins, on the other hand, believes it was caused by Mexican belligerency over the annexation of Texas.

[2] For a contemporary discussion of the alleged "slave-holding conspiracy" see William Jay, *A Review of the Causes and Consequences of the Mexican War* (Boston: Benjamin B. Mussey & Co., 1849), particularly Chapter 4. Ulysses S. Grant, who opposed the war despite the fact that he served in it, went so far as to contend that the Civil War was a sort of national punishment for the Mexican War. See Grant, *Personal Memoirs of U. S. Grant: Selected Letters, 1839–1865* (New York: Literary Classics of the United States, Inc., 1990), 42.

[3] Justo Sierra, "The Tragedy of 1846," reprinted in Ramón Eduardo Ruíz (ed.), *The Mexican War: Was It Manifest Destiny* (Hinsdale, Ill.: The Dryden Press, 1963), 113. In his thoroughly researched work, *The War with Mexico* (2 vols.; New York: The MacMillan Company, 1919), Justin Smith estimates the size of the Mexican army at approximately 32,000 men in 1845 (I, 157), compared to about 7,200 for the United States Army (I, 139). The Mexican figure, however, is disputed by William

A. DePaolo Jr. in *The Mexican National Army, 1822–1852* (College Station: Texas A&M University Press, 1997), 96, which gives the nominal strength as 18,882 permanent troops and 1,174 presidial (frontier) troops, although the presidials existed primarily on paper.

[4] Ramsey, *The Other Side*, 1–2.

[5] Alleine Howren, "Causes and Origin of the Decree of April 6, 1830," *Southwestern Historical Quarterly*, 16 (Apr., 1913), 378–381; K. Jack Bauer, *The Mexican War, 1846–1848* (Lincoln: University of Nebraska Press, 1992), 3; Ramsey, *The Other Side*, 3–4.

[6] Sierra, "The Tragedy of 1846," 112–113; Hubert Howe Bancroft, *History of Mexico* (6 vols.; San Francisco: The History Company, 1887), V, 151–152; Bauer, *The Mexican War*, 1–3.

[7] Glenn W. Price, *Origins of the War with Mexico: The Polk–Stockton Intrigue* (Austin: University of Texas Press, 1967), 15–25; Ramsey, *The Other Side*, 30–31 (quotation).

[8] John S. D. Eisenhower, *So Far from God: The U.S. War with Mexico, 1846–1848* (New York: Random House, 1989), xviii–xix, 18–19; Bauer, *The Mexican War*, 2. The term "manifest destiny" first appeared in an article entitled "Annexation," which appeared in the July–August 1845 issue of *United States Magazine and Democratic Review*, and accused "other nations," specifically Britain and France, of "the avowed object of thwarting our policy and hampering our power, limiting our greatness and checking the fulfillment of our manifest destiny to overspread the continent allotted by Providence for the free development of our yearly multiplying millions." For much of the twentieth century it was believed the article was written—and the term "manifest destiny" coined—by John L. O'Sullivan, who was editor of the *Democratic Review* at the time. Recently, however, historian Linda S. Hudson has made a strong case that the article was written by O'Sullivan's associate, Jane McManus Storm, an early advocate of social equality and expansionism, who wrote for the *Democratic Review* at the time. See Linda S. Hudson, *Mistress of Manifest Destiny: A Biography of Jane McManus Storm Cazneau, 1807–1878* (Austin: Texas State Historical Association, 2001), 58–62.

[9] Edward D. Mansfield, *The Mexican War: A History of Its Origin, and a Detailed Account of the Victories Which Terminated in the Surrender of the Capital; With the Official Dispatches of the Generals* (New York: A. S. Barnes & Co., 1848), iv. Seymour V. Connor and Odie B. Faulk raise the possibility that Great Britain worked to destabilize relations between Mexico and the United States. Unable to sustain a two-front war, the United States would be forced to compromise with Great Britain on the Oregon issue. Indeed, Polk's all-or-nothing stance on Oregon did not soften until hostilities had actually broken out with Mexico. Paredes, meanwhile, had been laboring under the impression that Britain would support Mexico in a war with the United States, an illusion that completely vanished following the Mexican defeats as Palo Alto and Resaca de la Palma. See Connor and Faulk, *North America Divided*, 136–138.

[10] Bauer, *The Mexican War*, 4, 17–18; Bancroft, *The History of Mexico*, V, 289; Smith, *The War with Mexico*, I, 87; Sierra, "The Tragedy of 1846," 113.

[11] In *Origins of the War with Mexico: The Polk–Stockton Intrigue*, Glenn W. Price raises the possibility that, from the very beginning, Polk conspired with Cmdre.

Robert F. Stockton to seize northern Mexico all the way to California by instigating a war in Texas. Bauer believes Stockton was in league with a pro-American war movement in Texas, but was operating independently and counter to Polk's agenda. See also Bauer, *The Mexican War*, 9–10.

[12] Allan Nevins (ed.), *Polk: The Diary of a President, 1845–1849, Covering the Mexican War, the Acquisition of Oregon, and the Conquest of California and the Southwest* (New York: Longmans, Green and Co., 1929), 10 (quotation); Ramsey, *The Other Side*, 34; U.S. Consul John Black to John Slidell, extracts, Dec. 15, 1845, in *Messages of the President of the United States With the Correspondence, Therewith Communicated, Between the Secretary of War and Other Officers of the Government, on the Subject of the Mexican War*, U.S. Congress, House of Representatives, 30th Cong., 1st sess., Executive Document no. 60 (Washington, D.C.: Wendell, and Van Benthuysen, Printers, 1848), 28–30 (hereafter cited as HED 60); Bauer, *The Mexican War*, 24–26. The three months of the Herrera administration and Paredes' insurrection are described in José Fernando Ramírez, *Mexico During the War with the United States* (Columbia: University of Missouri Press, 1950), chapter 1.

[13] Daniel R. Tilden, *Speech of Mr. Daniel R. Tilden, of Ohio, on the Mexican War Delivered in the House of Representatives, Tuesday, July 14, 1846* (Washington, D.C.: Office of Blair and Rives, 1846), 3; Eisenhower, *So Far from God*, xviii; Price, *Origins of the War with Mexico*, 5; Connor and Faulk, *North America Divided*, 135. Many Ohio citizens initially were opposed to the war but once hostilities commenced they embraced the cause with enthusiasm, sending three thousand troops within two weeks of the first call for volunteers. See Smith, *War with Mexico*, I, 195.

[14] Wayne Cutler, "President Polk's New England Tour: North for Union," in Douglas W. Richmond (ed.), *Essays on the Mexican War* (College Station: Texas A&M Press for the University of Texas at Arlington, 1986), 8–9.

2. "Hostilities . . . Have Been Commenced"

[1] Eisenhower, *So Far from God*, 30; Marcy to Taylor, May 28, 1845, HED 60, 79–81 (quotations).

[2] Eisenhower, *So Far from God*, 29–30; Grant, *Personal Memoirs*, 70 (quotation). Note: throughout this work, when an officer's rank and/or unit are not clear from other sources, they were verified in Francis B. Heitman, *Historical Register and Dictionary of the United States Army, From its Organization, September 29, 1789, to March 2, 1903* (2 vols.; Washington, D.C.: Government Printing Office, 1903), vol. I.

[3] Eisenhower, *So Far from God*, 30, 32; John Edward Weems, *To Conquer a Peace: The War between the United States and Mexico* (1974; reprint, College Station: Texas A&M University Press, 1988), 55–58; Marcy to Taylor, July 30, 1845, HED 60, 82–83; Taylor to Adjutant General, U.S. Army, Aug. 6, 1845, ibid., 83.

[4] Roger Jones, Adjutant General, U.S. Army, to Taylor, Aug. 6, 1845, HED 60, 83–84; Taylor to Anson Jones, Aug. 16, 1845, ibid., 101; Nevins, *Polk: The Diary of a President*, 11.

[5] Taylor to Adjutant General, U.S. Army, Sept. 14, 1845, HED 60, 107; W. W. S. Bliss, Assistant Adjutant General, Army of Occupation, to Hays, Sept. 12, 1845,

State of Texas, Office of the Adjutant General, RG 401, Texas Adjutant General's Files (Texas State Library and Archives, Austin).

[6] W. S. Henry, *Campaign Sketches of the War with Mexico* (New York: Harper & Brothers, Publishers, 1847), 26; Charles Robinson, *The Men Who Wear the Star: The Story of the Texas Rangers* (New York: Random House, 2000), 53; Andrew Jackson Sowell, *Life of "Big Foot" Wallace, the Great Ranger Captain* (new ed.; Austin: State House Press, 1989), 122; Grant, *Personal Memoirs*, 53.

[7] Taylor to Adjutant General, U.S. Army, Nov. 19, 1845, HED 60, 114; Frederick Wilkins, *The Highly Irregular Irregulars: Texas Rangers in the Mexican War* (Austin: Eakin Press, 1990), 24; Robinson, *Men Who Wear the Star*, 74–75.

[8] William F. Goetzmann (ed.), "Our First Foreign War," *American Heritage*, 17 (June, 1966), 87. Goetzmann's article is a collection of letters from Pvt. Barna Upton to his family from the time of his enlistment at the beginning of 1845 until his death in the battle for Mexico City on October 15, 1847.

[9] Henry, *Campaign Sketches*, 27.

[10] Henry, *Campaign Sketches*, 44–45; Bauer, *The Mexican War*, 34–35; Richard Bruce Winders, *Mr. Polk's Army: The American Military Experience in the Mexican War* (College Station: Texas A&M University Press, 1997), 120–121, 133.

[11] Marcy to Taylor, Jan. 13, 1846, HED 60, 90–91.

[12] Taylor to Adjutant General, U.S. Army, Feb. 4, 16 (quotation), and 26, 1846, all in HED 60, 116–117 (quotation on 117); Eisenhower, *So Far from God*, 50.

[13] Eisenhower, *So Far from God*, 50–51; Taylor to Adjutant General, U.S. Army, Feb. 26 and Mar. 8, 1846, both in HED 60, 117–119.

[14] Headquarters, Army of Occupation, Mar. 8, 1846, Order no. 30, HED 60, 120 (Spanish translation, 119).

[15] Robert Ryal Miller, *Shamrock and Sword: The Saint Patrick's Battalion in the U.S.–Mexican War* (Norman: University of Oklahoma Press, 1989), 161–162.

[16] Henry, *Campaign Sketches*, 52; Grant to Julia Dent, Mar. 3, 1846, in Grant, *Personal Memoirs*, 906.

[17] Ramsey, *The Other Side*, 30–31 (quotation on 31); Tilden, *Speech . . . on the Mexican War*, 6–7; McCaffrey, *Army of Manifest Destiny: The American Soldier in the Mexican War, 1846–1848* (New York: New York University Press, 1992), 5–6; N. C. Brooks, *A Complete History of the Mexican War: Its Causes, Conduct and Consequences.* (Philadelphia: Grigg, Elliot & Co., 1849), 100.

[18] U.S. Consul I. P. Shatzel to James Buchanan, secretary of state, July 18, 1846, U.S. Department of State, dispatches from United States consuls in Matamoros, 1826–1906, vols. 4–6, Jan. 1, 1840–Dec. 12, 1857, National Archives Microfilm Publication M281, roll 2 (Washington: National Archives and Records Service, 1964).

[19] Eisenhower, *So Far from God*, 53–54; Taylor to Adjutant General, U.S. Army, Mar. 21, 1846, HED 60, 123–124.

[20] The general-in-chief of the forces assembled against the enemy, HED 60, 127–129 (translation). The original Spanish appears on pages 126–127 and is substantially the same.

[21] Taylor to Adjutant General, U.S. Army, Mar. 21 and 25, 1846, HED 60, 124 and 129–130; Henry, *Campaign Sketches*, 61–63; Bauer, *The Mexican War*, 39.

[22] Bauer, *The Mexican War*, 39–40; Henry, *Campaign Sketches*, 65. Grant to Julia Dent, Mar. 29, 1846, in Grant, *Personal Memoirs*, 907.

[23] Bauer, *The Mexican War*, 40; minutes of an interview between Brig. Gen. W. J. Worth, U. S. Army, and [Brig.] Gen. Romulo [Díaz de la] Vega, of the Mexican army, held on the right bank of the Rio Grande, Mar. 28, 1846, HED 60, 134–138.

[24] Henry, *Campaign Sketches*, 65; Taylor to Adjutant General, U.S. Army, Mar. 29, 1846, and Apr. 6, 1846, HED 60, 132–133; Bauer, *The Mexican War*, 41–42. The history of the San Patricio Battalion is recorded by Robert Ryal Miller in *Shamrock and Sword*.

[25] Henry, *Campaign Sketches*, 73.

[26] Bauer, *The Mexican War*, 46–47; Ampudia to Taylor, Apr. 12, 1846, HED 60, 140.

[27] Henry, *Campaign Sketches*, 74–75.

[28] Bauer, *The Mexican War*, 46; Henry, *Campaign Sketches*, 77–79. A member of a distinguished naval family who opted for the army, Porter was the son of Cmdre. David Porter and brother of Rear Adm. David Dixon Porter, heroes of the War of 1812 and Civil War, respectively.

[29] Robinson, *Men Who Wear the Star*, 75; Brooks, *Complete History*, 108. Wilkins lists Walker's company as having ninety-one privates; see Wilkins, *Highly Irregular Irregulars*, 25. Brooks's figure is used because of timeliness of his account.

[30] Bauer, *The Mexican War*, 47; Eisenhower, *So Far from God*, 63; Ramsey, *The Other Side*, 39–40 n.

[31] Henry, *Campaign Sketches*, 84–85; Taylor to Adjutant General, U.S. Army, Apr. 26, 1846, HED 60, 288; Thornton to Taylor, Apr. 27, 1846, ibid., 290.

[32] Brooks, *Complete History*, 99–100 (quotation).

[33] Brooks, *Complete History*, 100.

3. The Opening Guns

[1] Smith, *War With Mexico*, I, 156–157; DePaolo, *Mexican National Army*, 72–73.

[2] Winders, *Mr. Polk's Army*, 9; Bernard de Voto, *The Year of Decision: 1846* (Boston: Little, Brown and Company, 1943), 203–206; Eisenhower, *So Far from God*, xxi–xxii.

[3] Grant, *Personal Memoirs*, 49–50; Winders, *Mr. Polk's Army*, 54–55; Eisenhower, *So Far from God*, 35.

[4] Winders, *Mr. Polk's Army*, 89, 92–100; Smith, *War with Mexico*, I, 156–157; DePaolo, *Mexican National Army*, 97.

[5] Winders, *Mr. Polk's Army*, 118–123; Smith, *War with Mexico*, I, 157.

[6] Eisenhower, *So Far from God*, 38, 62; Smith, *War with Mexico*, I, 158–159.

[7] Eisenhower, *So Far from God*, 73; Henry, *Campaign Sketches*, 83.

[8] Eisenhower, *So Far from God*, 74; Henry, *Campaign Sketches*, 85; Taylor to Adjutant General, U.S. Army, May 3, 1846, HED 60, 288–290; Brooks, *Mexican War*,

108–109; Nelson Lee, *Three Years among the Comanches* (1859; reprint, Norman: University of Oklahoma Press, 1991), 71–72.

[9] Taylor to Adjutant General, U.S. Army, May 3, 1846, HED 60, 289; Bauer, *The Mexican War*, 48–49; Ramsey, *The Other Side*, 42–44.

[10] Henry, *Campaign Sketches*, 88.

[11] Grant, *Personal Memoirs*, 65.

[12] This individual has also been called Sarah Bourdett. Apparently her official status was laundress, which made her military personnel. Nevertheless, regulations specified that laundresses could only accompany troops in the field if they were married, so she attached herself to a soldier of the Seventh Infantry named Borginnis, and was known by his name among the troops. Like many women in the laundry service, she casually changed partners as the mood or situation struck her, and continued to do so throughout the war. She seems to have been a favorite among the troops and undoubtedly was brave, tending the wounded and keeping the other camp women calm during the siege. See Eisenhower, *So Far From God*, 72–73, 76.

[13] Brown to W. W. S. Bliss, Assistant Adjutant General, Army of Occupation, May 4, 1846, HED 60, 293–294; Eisenhower, *So Far from God*, 75–76; John Frost, *Pictorial History of Mexico and the Mexican War: Comprising an Account of the Ancient Aztec Empire, the Conquest by Cortes, Mexico Under the Spaniards, the Mexican Revolution, the Republic, the Texan War, and the Recent War with the United States* (Philadelphia: Thomas, Cowperthwait and Co., 1849), 217.

[14] Taylor to Adjutant General, U.S. Army, May 5, 1846, HED 60, 293; Brown to Bliss, May 4, 1846, ibid., 294.

[15] Brown to Bliss, May 4, 1846, HED 6, 294; Ramsey, *The Other Side*, 45–46; Frost, *Pictorial History*, 218–219; Brooks, *Complete History*, 113–116.

[16] Brooks, *Complete History*, 116–118. Arista's note is reprinted on pages 117–118 and Hawkins's reply on page 118.

4. PALO ALTO AND RESACA DE LA PALMA

[1] Headquarters, Army of Occupation, May 7, 1846, Order no. 58, May 7, 1846, HED 60, 487.

[2] Henry, *Campaign Sketches*, 89–90.

[3] Ramsey, *The Other Side*, 43; Eisenhower, *So Far from God*, 73–74.

[4] Ramsey, *The Other Side*, 43.

[5] Henry, *Campaign Sketches*, 90.

[6] Henry, *Campaign Sketches*, 90; Goetzmann, "Our First Foreign War," 88.

[7] Ramsey, *The Other Side*, 45; *Campaña Contra los Americanos del Norte, Primera Parte, Relación Histórica de los Cuarenta Dias Qué Mandó en Gefe el Ejército del Norte el E. Sr. General de división don Mariano Arista; Escrita Por un Oficial de Infantería* (México: Imprenta de Ignacio Cumplido, 1846), 8–9; Eisenhower, *So Far from God*, 76–77.

[8] Ramsey, *The Other Side*, 46–47.

[9] Eisenhower, *So Far from God*, 77.

[10] Goetzmann, "Our First Foreign War," 89.

[11] Eisenhower, *So Far from God*, 77–79; Ramsey, *The Other Side*, 48n; Henry, *Campaign Sketches*, 93.

[12] Grant to Julia Dent, May 11, 1846, in Grant, *Personal Memoirs*, 910.

[13] Taylor to Adjutant General, U.S. Army, May 9, 1846, HED 60, 295; Henry, *Campaign Sketches*, 93–94; Eisenhower, *So Far from God*, 79.

[14] Ramsey, *The Other Side*, 50.

[15] *Campaña Contra los Americanos del Norte*, 15.

[16] Eisenhower, *So Far from God*, 81. Eisenhower cites several different accounts of this meeting.

[17] Henry, *Campaign Sketches*, 94–95.

[18] Ramsey, *The Other Side*, 50–51; *Campaña Contra los Americanos del Norte*, 16–17.

[19] Bauer, *The Mexican War*, 60; Eisenhower, *So Far from God*, 81–83.

[20] Henry, *Campaign Sketches*, 97.

[21] Henry, *Campaign Sketches*, 97; Brooks, *Complete History*, 143.

[22] Eisenhower, *So Far from God*, 83; Bauer, *The Mexican War*, 63.

[23] Grant, *Personal Memoirs*, 68–69.

[24] Eisenhower, *So Far from God*, 83–94.

[25] Frost, *Pictorial History*, 219–221.

[26] Headquarters, Army of Occupation, Orders no. 60, May 12, 1846, HED 60, 488.

[27] Headquarters, Army of Occupation, Orders no. 62, May 17, 1846, HED 60, 489; Taylor to Adjutant General, U.S. Army, May 12, 1846, ibid., 297; Brooks, *Complete History*, 150; Eisenhower, *So Far From God*, 84; Schatzel to Buchanan, July 18, 1846, dispatches from United States consuls in Matamoros.

5. OCCUPATION

[1] Nevins, *Polk: The Diary of a President*, 81–86, 89 (quotation on 81); Bauer, *The Mexican War*, 69.

[2] Nevins, *Polk: The Diary of a President*, 95.

[3] Nevins, *Polk: The Diary of a President*, 103–105; Eisenhower, *So Far from God*, 93–96.

[4] Taylor to Adjutant General, U.S. Army, May 18, 1846; May 26, 1846; June 2, 1846, and July 2, 1846, all in HED 60, 297, 298, 299, 305–306, 330–32; Bauer, *The Mexican War*, 81–82.

[5] Bauer, *The Mexican War*, 83.

[6] William Starr Myers (ed.), *The Mexican War Diary of George B. McClellan* (Princeton: Princeton University Press, 1917), 8–9.

[7] Goetzmann, "Our First Foreign War," 91–92; Winders, *Mr. Polk's Army*, 143–144, 151; S. Compton Smith, *Chile con Carne: Or, The Camp and Field* (New York: Miller and Curtis, 1857), 65.

[8] Lawrence Clayton and Joseph E. Chance (eds.), *The March to Monterrey: The Diary of Lt. Rankin Dilworth* (El Paso: Texas Western Press, 1996), 30.

[9] Winders, *Mr. Polk's Army*, 12–13; Bauer, *The Mexican War*, 70–72, 83; Henry, *Campaign Sketches*, 124.

[10] Bauer, *The Mexican War*, 85.

[11] Joseph E. Chance (ed.), *Mexico under Fire: Being the Diary of Samuel Ryan Curtis, 3rd Ohio Volunteer Regiment, During the American Military Occupation of Northern Mexico, 1846–1847* (Fort Worth: Texas Christian University Press, 1994), 30.

[12] Grant to Julia Dent, July 25, 1846, in Grant, *Personal Memoirs*, 918.

[13] Wilkins, *Highly Irregular Irregulars*, 36–41; John Caperton, "Sketch of Colonel John C. Hays, The Texas Rangers, Incidents in Texas and Mexico, Etc." (Center for American History, University of Texas at Austin), 42–43; Samuel C. Reid Jr., *The Scouting Expeditions of McCulloch's Texas Rangers: Or, The Summer and Fall Campaign of the Army of the United States in Mexico—1846* (1847; reprint, Austin: The Steck Company, 1935), 26.

[14] James K. Holland, "Diary of a Texan Volunteer in the Mexican War," *Southwestern Historical Quarterly*, 30, (July, 1926), 12; Reid, *Scouting Expeditions*, 61.

[15] Holland, "Diary of a Texan Volunteer," 12, 19.

[16] Mackenzie, whose name originally was Alexander Mackenzie Slidell, was brother of John Slidell, Polk's plenipotentiary, and father of Ranald Slidell Mackenzie, who would distinguish himself during the Indian Wars in Texas in the late 1860s and early 1870s. Alexander had reversed the order of his middle and last names in 1837 at the behest of a wealthy maternal uncle who wanted the name Mackenzie preserved.

[17] Nevins, *Polk: The Diary of a President*, 52; Bauer, *The Mexican War*, 76–77.

[18] Justin Smith (ed.), "Letters of General Antonio Lopez de Santa Anna Relating to the War Between the United States and Mexico, 1846–1848," *Annual Report of the American Historical Association for the Year 1917* (Washington, D.C.: [Government Printing Office], 1920), 358. Smith's editing is rudimentary. The letters are not translated, and often the recipient is not specified. Consequently, they are cited by page number only and not by sender/recipient or date. See also Bauer, *The Mexican War*, 77.

[19] Ejército Liberador Republicano.

[20] Smith, "Letters of General Antonio Lopez de Santa Anna," 363 n.10.

[21] Reid, *Scouting Expeditions*, 46–47; Clayton and Chance, *March to Monterrey*, 36.

[22] Clayton and Chance, *March to Monterrey*, 35. Reid, *Scouting Expeditions*, 66.

[23] Taylor to Adjutant General, U.S. Army, Aug. 3, 1846, HED 60, 402.

[24] Reid, *Scouting Expeditions*, 68–74.

[25] Taylor to Adjutant General, U.S. Army, Aug. 10, 1846; Taylor to Wool, Aug. 14, 1846; Taylor to Adjutant General, U.S. Army, Aug. 19, 1846, all in HED 60, 408, 410–412.

6. MONTERREY

[1] Connor and Faulk, *North America Divided*, 136, 144–146,156.

[2] John H. Schroeder, *Mr. Polk's War: American Opposition and Dissent, 1846–1848* (Madison: University of Wisconsin Press, 1973), 37–38.

[3] Homer Wilbur (James Russell Lowell), *The Biglow Papers, Edited, With an Introduction, Notes, Glossary, and Copious Index, by Homer Wilbur, A.M., Pastor of the First Church in Jaalam, and (Prospective) Member of Many Literary, Learned and Scientific Societies* (Cambridge: George Nichols, 1848), 4, 9–11.

[4] Schroder, *Mr. Polk's War*, 37.

[5] Schroeder, *Mr. Polk's War*, 22–24; John C. Calhoun to Henry W. Conner, May 15, 1846, ibid., 24 (quotation).

[6] Eisenhower, *So Far from God*, 120–121.

[7] Eisenhower, *So Far from God*, 120–122; Bauer, *The Mexican War*, 90; Taylor to Adjutant General, U.S. Army, Sept. 12, 1846, HED 60, 421; Henry, *Campaign Sketches*, 178–179.

[8] General-in-chief of the Army of the North, Aug. 31, 1846, HED 60, 421; General-in-chief of the Army of the North, circular, Sept. 5, 1846, ibid., 422–423; Clayton and Chance, *March to Monterrey*, 65; Miller, *Shamrock and Sword*, 44–45.

[9] Clayton and Chance, *March to Monterrey*, 68.

[10] Clayton and Chance, *March to Monterrey*, 69. Dilworth died on September 27.

[11] Bauer, *The Mexican War*, 90–92; Holland, "Diary of a Texan Volunteer," 25; Wilkins, *Highly Irregular Irregulars*, 83.

[12] Holland, "Diary of a Texan Volunteer," 25.

[13] Carlos Pérez Maldonado, "El Obispado," in Lourdes Islas (comp.), *El Obispado a Través de la Historia* (México, D.F.: Asociación de Amigos del Museo del Obispado, A.C., 1999), 15–52, 19.

[14] Henry, *Campaign Sketches*, 192–193; Bauer, *The Mexican War*, 93–97; Eisenhower, *So Far from God*, 127–130.

[15] Bauer, *The Mexican War*, 97; Sowell, *Life of "Big Foot" Wallace*, 122–123.

[16] Bauer, *The Mexican War*, 97; Holland, "Diary of a Texan Volunteer," 26; Eisenhower, *So Far from God*, 141; Stephen B. Oates, "The Texas Rangers in the Mexican War," *Texas Military History*, 3 (Summer, 1963), 65–85, 68; James Buckner Barry, *Buck Barry, Texas Ranger and Frontiersman* (new ed.; Lincoln: University of Nebraska Press, 1984), 38.

[17] Barry, *Buck Barry*, 38–39.

[18] Goetzmann, "Our First Foreign War," 95.

[19] Bauer, *The Mexican War*, 99; Oates, "Texas Rangers in the Mexican War," 68.

[20] Brooks, *Complete History*, 188–189; Bauer, *The Mexican War*, 99. Davis had married Taylor's daughter, Sarah Knox Taylor, in the spring of 1835. That summer, however, she died of malaria. At the time of the Mexican War, Davis was married to Varina Howell.

[21] Brooks, *Complete History*, 191–192; Nevins, *Polk: The Diary of a President*, 155 n.2.

[22] Henry, *Campaign Sketches* 223–224.

7. Buena Vista

[1] James M. McCaffrey (ed.), *"Surrounded by Dangers of All Kinds": The Mexican War Letters of Lieutenant Theodore Laidley* (Denton: University of North Texas Press, 1997), 24; Chance, *Mexico under Fire*, 42.

[2] Chance, *Mexico under Fire*, 39.

[3] Ibid., 39–40.

[4] Nevins, *Polk: The Diary of a President*, 155–156.

[5] Taylor to Adjutant General, U.S. Army, Oct. 11, 1846; statement of Lt. W. B. P. Gaines, with endorsement by John C. Hays, Oct. 6, 1846; Taylor to Adjutant General, U.S. Army, Oct. 6, 1846 (quotation), all HED 60, 430–432. Some Mexican military personnel were allowed to remain in Monterrey to see to that army's wounded. See Smith, "Letters of General Antonio Lopez de Santa Anna," 392 n.5.

[6] Smith, "Letters of General Antonio Lopez de Santa Anna," 368; Taylor to Santa Anna, Nov. 5, 1846, HED 60, 437; Taylor to Adjutant General, U.S. Army, Nov. 9, 1846, ibid., 361.

[7] Bauer, *The Mexican War*, 202–204.

[8] Henry, *Campaign Sketches*, 294.

[9] Bauer, *The Mexican War*, 201, 204–206; Smith, "Letters of General Antonio Lopez de Santa Anna," 399.

[10] Nevins, *Polk: The Diary of a President*, 163; Marcy to Taylor, Oct. 22, 1846, HED 60, 362 (1st quotation); Marcy to Scott, Nov. 23, 1846, ibid., 836–837; Scott to Taylor, Dec. 20, 1846, ibid., 839–840 (2nd quotation).

[11] Mansfield, *The Mexican War*, 118.

[12] Taylor to Adjutant General, U.S. Army, Jan. 26, 1847, HED 60, 1099; Bauer, *The Mexican War*, 206–207; Chance, *Mexico under Fire*, 148; Mansfield, *The Mexican War*, 121.

[13] Taylor to Adjutant General, U.S. Army, HED 60, 1099; Wilkins, *Highly Irregular Irregulars*, 123–125; Chance, *Mexico under Fire*, 113; J. Frank Dobie, "Mustang Gray: Fact, Tradition, and Song," *Tone the Bell Easy*, Publications of the Texas Folklore Society no. 10 (1932), 109–112; Samuel Chamberlain, *My Confession: Recollections of a Rogue* (Austin: Texas State Historical Association, 1996), 6, 10.

[14] Bauer, *The Mexican War*, 206–207; Eisenhower, *So Far From God*, 181; Brooks, *Complete History*, 205; Wool to Bliss, Jan. 27, 1847, HED 60, 1106–1108; Taylor to Adjutant General. U.S. Army, ibid., 1109–1110.

[15] Brooks, *Complete History*, 203–205; Eisenhower, *So Far from God*, 179–182; Ramsey, *The Other Side*, 120–121.

[16] Santa Anna to Taylor, Feb. 22, 1847, reprinted in Brooks, *Complete History*, 208.

[17] Chamberlain, *My Confession*, 155.

[18] Taylor to Santa Anna, Feb. 22, 1847, reprinted in Brooks, *Complete History*, 209.

[19] Ramsey, *The Other Side*, 122; Eisenhower, *So Far from God*, 183–186.

[20] Eisenhower, *So Far from God*, 187–188; Brooks, *Complete History*, 212–216.

[21] Eisenhower, *So Far from God*, 188–189; Mansfield, *The Mexican War*, 124 (quotation); Brooks, *Complete History*, 216–218.

[22] Eisenhower, *So Far from God*, 188–191.

[23] Bauer, *The Mexican War*, 218; Chance, *Mexico under Fire*, 148.

[24] Eisenhower, *So Far from God*, 190; Taylor to Marcy, Mar. 6, 1847 (quotation), reprinted in Mansfield, *The Mexican War*, 137.

[25] Nevins, *Polk: The Diary of a President*, 208–209.

[26] Bauer, *The Mexican War*, 208.

[27] Mirabeau B. Lamar, *Papers of Mirabeau Buonaparte Lamar* (6 vols.; Austin: A. C. Baldwin and Sons, vols. 1–2; Austin: Von Boeckmann-Jones, Inc., vols. 3–6, 1921–1927), IV, part 1, 167–168; Dobie, "Mustang Gray," 112.

[28] Walter Paye Lane, *The Adventures and Recollections of General Walter P. Lane* (Austin: Jenkins Publishing Co./Pemberton Press, 1970), 53–59.

[29] Taylor to Adjutant General, U.S. Army, June 16, 1847, HED 60, 1178.

8. Texans with Scott

[1] Heitman, *Historical Register*, I, 997; R. L. Wilson, *Colt, An American Legend: The Official History of Colt Firearms from 1836 to the Present* (sesquicentennial ed.; New York: Abbeville Press, 1985), 23–28; Samuel Colt to Samuel H. Walker, Jan. 18, 1847, Samuel Hamilton Walker Papers (Texas State Library and Archives, Austin); Robinson, *Men Who Wear the Star*, 93–94.

[2] Robinson, *Men Who Wear the Star*, 94; John Salmon Ford, *Rip Ford's Texas*, ed. Stephen B. Oates (Austin: University of Texas Press, 1963; reprint, 1994), 87 n.1 (quotation).

[3] Wilkins, *Highly Irregular Irregulars*, 155, 163.

[4] Samuel H. Walker to Jonathan T. Walker, Oct. 5, 1847, Walker Papers.

[5] Eisenhower, *So Far from God*, 348–349; Jenkins, *History of the War with Mexico*, 464–465; Wilkins, *Highly Irregular Irregulars*, 165.

[6] James K. Greer, *Colonel Jack Hays: Texas Frontier Leader and California Builder* (rev. ed.; Waco: W. M. Morrison, 1973), 170; Ford, *Rip Ford's Texas*, 70. Ford always wrote in the third person.

[7] Greer, *Colonel Jack Hays*, 170–172.

[8] Ford, *Rip Ford's Texas*, 79; Wilkins, *Highly Irregular Irregulars*, 166–168.

[9] Ford, *Rip Ford's Texas*, 83.

[10] Ford, *Rip Ford's Texas*, 83–84; Connor and Faulk, *North America Divided*, 131–132.

INDEX

Illustrations are noted in *italics*.

Adams, John Quincy, 3
Alcaráz, Ramón, 94 n.1
Allsens, Adam, 91
Ampudia, Pedro de, 23, 25, 35, 37, 72–74; described, 25; at Monterrey, 61–62, 68–70; at Buena Visa, 80–81
Angostura. See Buena Vista.
Apuntes para la historia de la Guerra entre México y los Estados Unidos (book), 94 n.1
Arista, Mariano, 25, 35–37, *38*, 42–43, 56, 62, 74; described, 25; crosses Rio Grande, 31; at Palo Alto, 39–41; at Resaca de la Palma, 44, 46

Belknap, William Goldsmith, 45, 92
Barry, James Buckner (Buck), 68
Bauer, K. Jack, 95–96 n.11
Biglow Papers (book), 60
Bishop's Palace (Monterrey defense), 63–68, *65*, 73
Black Fort (Monterrey defense). See Citadel
Blanco, Santiago, 80–81
Bliss, William Wallace Smith, 24, 80, 92
Borginnis, Sarah, *32*, 34, 99 n.12
Bourdett, Sarah. See Borginnis, Sarah.
Bragg, Braxton, 36, 81–82
Bravo, Nicolás, 56

Briggs, George, 60
Brooks, Nathaniel Covington, 1, 94 n.1
Brown, Jacob, 31–32, 34–35, *36*, 92; mortally wounded, 36; death of, 46
Buena Vista, 7, 23, 63, 73, 76, 78–83; Santa Anna's strategy for, 76; Mexican strength at, 76, 79; terrain of, 78, 80; U.S. losses at, 82–83
Buffalo Hump (Comanche), 57
Butler, William, 78

Calhoun, John C., 61
Camp Belknap, Tex., 23, 43
"Camp Opposite Matamoras." See Fort Brown.
Canales, Antonio, 44, 83
Carricitos. See Thornton's Skirmish.
Casa Mata (blockhouse in Matamoros), 29, 63
Casualties, U.S., 2
Centralists (Mexican political faction), 5
Cerro Gordo, 7
Chadbourne, Theodore Lincoln, 92
Chamberlain, Samuel, 80
Chapultepec, 63
Churubusco, 63
Citadel (Monterrey defense), 61, 64, 66, 68, 70, 73